Editor
Eric Migliaccio

Editorial Project Manager
Ina Massler Levin, M.A.

Editor in Chief
Sharon Coan, M.S. Ed.

Illustrator
Wendy Chang

Cover Artist
Jessica Orlando

Art Coordinator
Denice Adorno

Creative Director
Elayne Roberts

Imaging
Rosa C. See

Product Manager
Phil Garcia

Publishers
Rachelle Cracchiolo, M.S. Ed.
Mary Dupuy Smith, M.S. Ed.

MEETING
WRITING
STANDARDS

Story Writing

Grades 1-2

Written by

Sarah Kartchner Clark, M.A.

Teacher
Created
Materials

Teacher Created Materials, Inc.
6421 Industry Way
Westminster, CA 92683
www.teachercreated.com
ISBN-1-57690-982-4
©2000 Teacher Created Materials, Inc.
Made in U.S.A.

Table of Contents

Introduction

You are about to embark on a unit of story writing. This unit is geared especially for students in first and second grade or students at similar levels. Story writing is a fun and easy way to acquire writing skills. The lessons and activities in this unit are written to give students plenty of practice and opportunities to become familiar with the steps of the writing process and writing a story.

The Story-Writing Unit

This unit has been divided into sections. Dividing this unit of study into sections will make it easier to focus on and assess each part of the story-writing process. The sections are as follows: Elements of Story Writing, The Writing Process, Create a Story, Types of Stories, Bring a Story to Life!, Story-Writing Learning Centers, and Mechanics and Grammar.

There are a variety of lessons in each section. You may choose to do all the lessons for each section, or you may select the lessons appropriate for the level of your students and your time frame. A unit planning sheet (page 4) has been included for your convenience as you plan the lessons and activities for this unit.

The Classroom Tips Section

In the "Classroom Tips" section of this book, you will find tips to help organize and prepare for the story-writing unit. It is important for you to make preparations ahead of time for the unit. Look on page 17 for daily doses to incorporate into the unit. You will find the bulletin board ideas on pages 12–15. There are bulletin board examples and ideas that will help reinforce the skills being taught in the lessons. Select the bulletin boards you will be using and get materials ready for each of them.

Also included in this section are technology connections (page 16), journal writing topics (page 18), a writing activity calendar (pages 10 and 11), parent and child activities (page 9), and a parent letter (page 8) to send home with activity suggestions and information about this unit. All of these features will add to your students' learning of story writing.

The Assessment Section

Assessment is critical in this unit. Writing a story is a perfect example of a student going through a process to reach a finished product. Assessment needs to take place at each step of the story-writing process. Portfolios are a great way to keep track of student progress and student work. Information on portfolio assessment is provided on page 19.

Assessment rubrics are provided at the end of each section. They are a form of assessment that will help you see how well your students are learning and mastering the standards and benchmarks. The teacher checklist on pages 20 and 21 is another form of assessment used in this unit. Another form of assessment in this unit involves student samples. Samples (page 23) of how students in first and second grades can write stories are provided as guides.

The final type of assessment included in this book is skill evaluation (page 22). This assessment will assist you when you are grading a story and looking at just one specific skill on which you are working with individual students. This type of assessment is used in the stages of brainstorming, drafting, editing, and revising.

Unit Planning Sheet

Date	Standard	Lesson #	Materials Needed

Learning Centers/Materials	Other Resources Needed
Games	

Standards for Writing
Grades K–2

Accompanying the major activities of this book will be references to the basic standards and benchmarks for writing that will be met by successful performance of the activities. Each specific standard and benchmark will be referred to by the appropriate letter and number from the following collection. For example, a basic standard and benchmark identified as **1A** would be as follows:

> **Standard 1:** Demonstrates competence in the general skills and strategies of the writing process
>
> **Benchmark A: Prewriting:** Uses prewriting strategies to plan written work (e.g., discusses ideas with peers, draws pictures to generate ideas, writes key thoughts and questions, rehearses ideas, records reactions and observations)

A standard and benchmark identified as **4B** would be as follows:

> **Standard 4:** Gathers and uses information for research purposes
>
> **Benchmark B:** Uses books to gather information for research topics (e.g., uses table of contents, examines pictures and charts)

Clearly, some activities will address more than one standard. Moreover, since there is a rich supply of activities included in this book, some will overlap in the skills they address, and some, of course, will not address every single benchmark within a given standard. Therefore, when you see these standards referenced in the activities, refer to this section for complete descriptions.

Although virtually every state has published its own standards and every subject area maintains its own lists, there is surprising commonality among these various sources. For the purposes of this book, we have elected to use the collection of standards synthesized by John S. Kendall and Robert J. Marzano in their book *Content Knowledge: A Compendium of Standards and Benchmarks for K–12 Education* (1997) as illustrative of what students at various grade levels should know and be able to do. The book is published jointly by McREL (Mid-continent Regional Educational Laboratory, Inc.) and ASCD (Association for Supervision and Curriculum Development). (Used by permission of McREL.)

Language Arts Standards

1. Demonstrates competence in the general skills and strategies of the writing process

2. Demonstrates competence in the stylistic and rhetorical aspects of writing

3. Uses grammatical and mechanical conventions in written compositions

4. Gathers and uses information for research purposes

Standards for Writing
Grades K–2 *(cont.)*

1. Demonstrates competence in the general skills and strategies of the writing process

A. Prewriting: Uses prewriting strategies to plan written work (e.g., discusses ideas with peers, draws pictures to generate ideas, writes key thoughts and questions, rehearses ideas, records reactions and observations)

B. Drafting and Revising: Uses strategies to draft and revise written work (e.g., rereads; rearranges words, sentences, and paragraphs to improve or clarify meaning; varies sentence types; adds descriptive words and details; deletes extraneous information; incorporates suggestions from peers and teachers; sharpens the focus)

C. Editing and Publishing: Uses strategies to edit and publish written work (e.g., proofreads using a dictionary and other resources; edits for grammar, punctuation, capitalization, and spelling at a developmentally appropriate level; incorporates illustrations or photos; shares finished product)

D. Evaluates own and others' writing (e.g., asks questions and makes comments about writing, helps classmates apply grammatical and mechanical conventions)

E. Dictates or writes with a logical sequence of events (e.g., includes a beginning, middle, and ending)

F. Dictates or writes detailed descriptions of familiar persons, places, objects, or experiences

G. Writes in response to literature

H. Writes in a variety of formats (e.g., picture books, letters, stories, poems, and information pieces)

2. Demonstrates competence in the stylistic and rhetorical aspects of writing

A. Uses general, frequently used words to convey basic ideas

Standards for Writing
Grades K-2 *(cont.)*

3. Uses grammatical and mechanical conventions in written compositions

    A. Forms letters in print and spaces words and sentences

    B. Uses complete sentences in written compositions

    C. Uses declarative and interrogative sentences in written compositions

    D. Uses nouns in written compositions (e.g., nouns for simple objects, family members, community workers, and categories)

    E. Uses verbs in written compositions (e.g., verbs for a variety of situations, action words)

    F. Uses adjectives in written compositions (e.g., uses descriptive words)

    G. Uses adverbs in written compositions (e.g., uses words that answer how, when, where, and why questions)

    H. Uses conventions of spelling in written compositions (e.g., spells high frequency, commonly misspelled words from appropriate grade-level list; uses a dictionary and other resources to spell words; spells own first and last names)

    I. Uses conventions of capitalization in written compositions (e.g., first and last names, first word of a sentence, etc.)

    J. Uses conventions of punctuation in written compositions (e.g., uses periods after declarative sentences, uses question marks after interrogative sentences, uses commas in a series)

4. Gathers and uses information for research purposes

    A. Generates questions about topics of personal interest

    B. Uses books to gather information for research topics (e.g., uses table of contents, examines pictures and charts)

Parent Letter

Dear Parents,

We are embarking on a new unit of study in the classroom. We will be learning how to write a story. Students will go through the writing process of brainstorming, writing a draft, editing, and revising to produce a finished product. There are many skills that your child will learn in this process. The following is a list of standards and benchmarks that your child will be taught:

1. **Demonstrates competence in the general skills and strategies of the writing process**
   A. Prewriting: Uses prewriting strategies to plan written work
   B. Drafting and Revising: Uses strategies to draft and revise written work
   C. Editing and Publishing: Uses strategies to edit and publish written work
   D. Evaluates own and others' writing
   E. Dictates or writes with a logical sequence of events
   F. Dictates or writes detailed descriptions of familiar persons, places, objects, or experiences
   G. Writes in response to literature
   H. Writes in a variety of formats

2. **Demonstrates competence in the stylistic and rhetorical aspects of writing.**
   A. Uses general, frequently used words to convey basic ideas

3. **Uses grammatical and mechanical conventions in written compositions**
   A. Forms letters in print and spaces words and sentences
   B. Uses complete sentences in written compositions
   C. Uses declarative and interrogative sentences in written compositions
   D. Uses nouns in written compositions
   E. Uses verbs in written compositions
   F. Uses adjectives in written compositions
   G. Uses adverbs in written compositions
   H. Uses conventions of spelling in written compositions
   I. Uses conventions of capitalization in written compositions
   J. Uses conventions of punctuation in written compositions

4. **Gathers and uses information for research purposes**
   A. Generates questions about topics of personal interest
   B. Uses books to gather information for research topics

We will be creating an editing center in the classroom. This center will include a number of reference materials. If possible, locate a dictionary at home that your child can use for homework assignments.

A calendar and a list of activities that you can do with your child will be sent home. These activities at home are meant to enrich this story-writing unit and to help parents be more involved in the learning process. If you have any questions, please don't hesitate to ask.

Sincerely,

_____

Parent and Child Activities

Dear Parents,

Here are some story-writing activities that you can do at home. These activities will enrich objectives and lessons being taught in school. If you have any questions, please don't hesitate to ask.

Sincerely,

_____

A Story a Day

Plan to read at least one story to your child every day. This can be a short story, or it can be a chapter book where a chapter is read each night. Set aside a specific time to read each day. As you read the story, notice who the author is, point out character traits, and encourage your child to look for the conflict and the resolution. Ask your child to make predictions as you read the story. All of this involvement will teach story organization, as well as create fond memories of reading for your child.

Parent-Child Story

For this activity, you are going to need paper and a pencil. Work with your child to write a story together. Decide the best way to do it, based on your personalities and strengths. Will you write a part and then let your child write a part, alternating back and forth? or will you decide the plot together as you go along? If your child has a difficult time writing, you be the scribe. Don't let that be a hindrance. When you have finished the story, enlist your child's help with the illustrations and "publish" it by writing it neatly on pages that are stapled together. It will be a treasure you can read and share for years to come!

Ideas on the Loose

Find ideas for stories by looking around your neighborhood, your park, your school, and your town. Choose one story to brainstorm about as a family a few minutes before bed. Who would be the characters? Where would the story take place? How would the story begin and end?

It's in the Bag

Place a variety of miscellaneous items in a bag. Invite your family to help you tell a story using the items in the bag. Begin the story by pulling out an item and using it in the story. Then have the next family member take out an object and add to the story. Play continues this way until all the items have been used and the story is finished.

In the Spotlight

Throughout this unit, your child will be asked to bring home a story to share with the family. Read the story together with your child. Then offer positive feedback on the story and on the writing abilities of your child. Spend time planning a way to put on a show of the story your child wrote. This could be a puppet show, a play, a reader's theater, or a videotaped performance. Encourage creativity in your child. Invite family members and friends to watch the show.

Writing Activity Calendar

Day 1 Go to the library and check out a book.	**Day 2** Read your library book today.	**Day 3** Read a fantasy story today.	**Day 4** Tell a friend about your favorite book.
Day 8 Find the setting in a book.	**Day 9** Read a book with a family member.	**Day 10** Make up a new ending to your favorite story.	**Day 11** Take a photo of a scene that could be from your story.
Day 14 Invite the principal to come read a story to your class.		**Day 15** Draw a picture of a scene in a book.	**Day 16** Write a pretend letter to a character in a book.
Day 20 Read a book with your dad.	**Day 21** Discuss with a friend a story you read.	**Day 22** Write a story about when you were a baby.	
Day 26 Read one of your stories to a younger child.	**Day 27** Collect all the stories you've written and pick your favorite.	**Day 28** Make a bookmark to use when you read.	**Day 29** Type a story on the computer.

10

Writing Activity Calendar *(cont.)*

Day 5 Write a letter to your favorite author.	**Day 6** Read a mystery book.	**Day 7** Make a snack that a character you've read about would eat.
Day 12 Have a dress-as-your-favorite-character day.		**Day 13** Watch a movie version of a book you've read. Compare the two.
Day 17 Count how many stories you have read since Day 1.	**Day 18** Read one of your stories aloud to the class.	**Day 19** Ask a family member to tell you about his/her favorite story.
Day 23 Ask your mom about her favorite story.	**Day 24** Act out a part from a story you've written.	**Day 25** Read a book outdoors today.
	Day 30 Make a book to give away.	**Day 31** Write 10 reasons why you are a good author.

Bulletin Board Ideas

Displaying your students' work throughout the unit can be good reinforcement for the skills they will be learning. Use the bulletin board ideas on the next few pages to highlight the different stages of the story-writing process: brainstorming, researching, drafting, editing, and publishing.

Bulletin Board #1

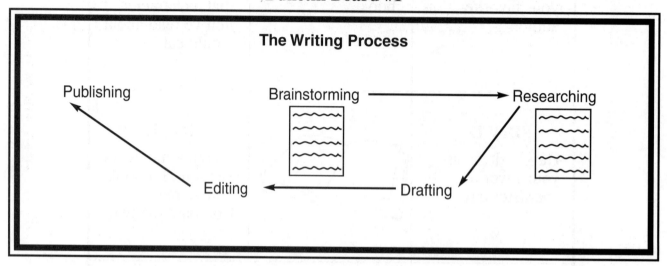

This bulletin board will show a work in progress! Put colorful paper up as a background and select a colorful border to put up around the edges. Across the top, staple large cutout letters to read "The Writing Process" and the words "Brainstorming," "Researching," "Drafting," "Editing," and "Publishing." Add arrows to show the writing process. Staple samples of student work from each category as students complete them.

Bulletin Board #2

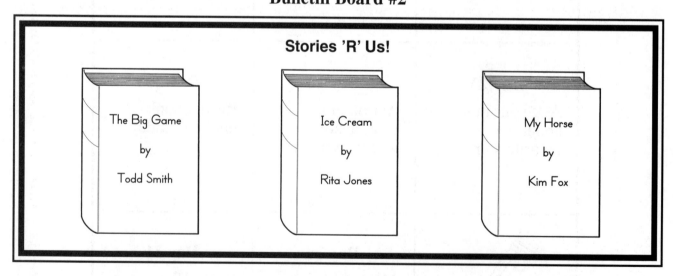

This bulletin board will display stories in the works. Put colorful paper up as a background and select a colorful border to put up around the edges. Make copies of the book pattern on page 13. Have each student cut out one and write the title of the story and his/her name on it. Staple the books with the students' stories onto the bulletin board. Across the top, staple large cutout letters to read "Stories 'R' Us!"

Bulletin Board Ideas *(cont.)*

Book Pattern

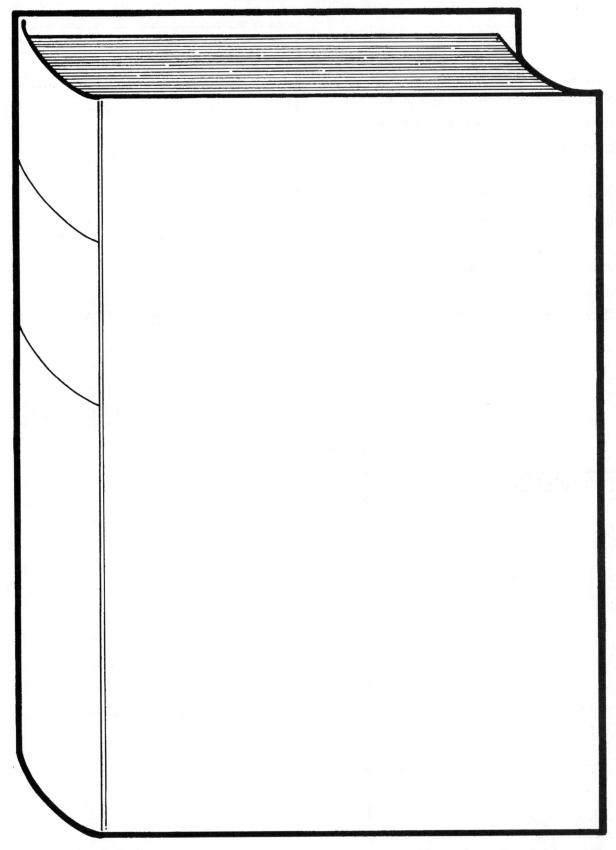

Bulletin Board Ideas *(cont.)*

Bulletin Board #3

This bulletin board will be a delicious way to reinforce sequencing! Put up colorful paper as a background and select a colorful border to put up around the edges. In large letters across the top, staple cutout letters to read "You Scream, I Scream . . . We All Scream for Ice Cream!" Make copies of the ice-cream cone on colored paper. Have students write each section of their stories on a different scoop of ice cream.

Bulletin Board #4

This bulletin board will display stories in the works. Put colorful paper up as a background and select a colorful border to put up around the edges. Make copies of the talk-bubble pattern on page 15. Have students cut out one and write a quote from one of their characters inside the talk bubble. This will give students practice with punctuation. Staple the talk bubbles onto the bulletin board. In large letters across the top, staple cutout letters to read

"What Did They Say?"

Bulletin Board Ideas *(cont.)*

Ice-Cream Cone and Talk Bubble Patterns

Technology Connections

There are ample opportunities to teach computer and technology skills while teaching the story-writing unit. This page lists technology activities that can be used with any lesson. Add them to each lesson in this unit, as needed. It is important to teach your students how to use the computer for research assignments. See the bibliography on page 143 for information on useful Web pages and Internet addresses.

Word Processing

Using a word-processing program, students can type their stories. Show students how to center and space the words. Students may use the computer to brainstorm their ideas, write their drafts, edit and revise their work, and/or publish their final drafts.

Spell Checker

Teach students how to use spell checker after they have finished typing their stories into the computer. Be sure to discuss with them how the computer may miss certain words that are spelled correctly but used incorrectly (as in the sentence *I know I am write about this*).

Printer Savvy

Once students have finished learning to type into the computer, actually seeing a printed version of what they produced on the computer can be exciting for them. Be sure to discuss with students proper ways to use the printer so as not to have paper jams, etc. Set up the procedure for your class. You may choose to not have students try to fix any jams or errors.

Graphic Design

With the help of *Corel Draw*, *Kid Pix*, or other computer drawing programs, have students use a computer to draw pictures of their animals.

Internet Research

With guided help and direction, students will be able to find many resources of interest on the Internet. On the day that you plan to use the Internet, have parents on hand to assist students in using search engines and finding different story resources on the Web.

Encyclopedias Online

There are many encyclopedias available as computer programs, as well as encyclopedias that can be found online.

Dictionary and Thesaurus.Com

Show students how to look up words by using dictionaries and thesauruses found online.

Writing Programs

There are many writing programs, such as *School House Rock,* that can help reinforce writing skill as well as provide easy-to-use formats for word processing.

Daily Doses

This section of the unit provides opportunities for the students to share what they are learning in the story-writing process. Daily doses are sprinkled throughout the day and are not part of a lesson or instruction given on story writing. These quick and fun activities are meant to be varied and done at different times each day. This will keep them from seeming mundane or routine. Use the suggestions below or create some of your own.

Spin a Story

Unfold a class story by telling a part of the story each day. Begin the first day by saying the title and introducing the first part of the story. The next day, assign another student to add to your story beginning. The following day, another student adds to the story. The story continues to grow each day with a new student adding a piece to the story. Continue this way until every student has had a turn/day to add to the story. On the final day of the story, add a conclusion or come up with an ending by discussing it as a class. After you have finished the story, ask the students to name their favorite part, an interesting character, and so forth. Reliving the story together as a class can be fun and can reinforce memory and comprehension skills.

Crazy Characters

Designate an area of your classroom wall as the "Crazy Character Corner." Post a large piece of paper in this corner or wall space. Any time a student finds a word that can be used to describe a character, write it on the paper. Students may also draw pictures of different characters. This will help students as they need words to help describe their characters.

Story Star

Place a star made of construction paper on a different student's desk each morning before students come into class. The student with the star on his or her desk gets to share with the class a story he or she is writing. The student can share a character or a part of the story; he or she may even want to share the title. Students will be excited to see who the lucky person is each morning.

Question at the Door

Every morning before your students walk into the classroom, post a question on the door of your classroom. The question might be related to a specific story, or it might be a general question. This activity will get students thinking the minute they walk through the door. Look at the examples below:

- Is your main character a girl or a boy?
- What book gives the definitions of words?
- What is your favorite story?
- What is your story about?

Show and Tell a Story

Instead of having students bring in toys or other items to share, have students bring in their favorite stories to read and share with the class. Students may read the stories, show pictures, and share favorite parts and favorite characters. These "book talks" will not only encourage other students to read these books, but they will also give students ideas for their own story-writing efforts.

Journal Writing

Allowing students to talk and write about their stories will help cement concepts and objectives. At the beginning of the unit, distribute or make notebooks for students to use. At a specified time of the day, have students respond to a topic in their journals. Listed below are journal topics. You and your students may also have other ideas to add to the list. Feel free to modify topics as needed.

1. The thing I like about my story is . . .

2. The part I haven't figured out yet in my story is . . .

3. The new thing I have learned while writing this story is . . .

4. The thing I wish I could change about my main character is . . .

5. The hardest thing about writing this story is . . .

6. I think a good writer . . .

7. The things I like to write stories about are . . .

8. Some of the things that make me a good writer are . . .

9. Some of the things I need to work on in my writing are . . .

10. The things I don't like writing about are . . .

11. The best story I've ever written is . . .

12. The type of story I most like to write is . . .

13. The type of story I most like to read is . . .

14. Something I learned about myself and writing is . . .

15. If I wrote a letter to an author, I would ask . . .

16. Kids need to write more stories because . . .

17. I think my writing is important when . . .

18. The thing I learned the most about when writing this story was . . .

19. I wish I could write a story about . . .

Portfolio Assessment

Because writing a story is a process, using a portfolio is the best way to show student progress. Portfolios allow students a means to demonstrate their understanding of each step in the writing process. A portfolio is simple to put together. A portfolio is made with a three-ring folder or binder. There needs to be a portfolio for each student. Write the name of the student on the outside of the folder so it can be easily identified. Keep the portfolios in a basket or box on a counter so you and your students can access them easily. Keep samples of student work throughout this story-writing unit. Be sure to include samples of each stage in the writing process, including prewriting, drafting, editing, revising, and publishing.

Keep the Following Points in Mind When Using Portfolios:

❏ The portfolio belongs to the student. Encourage students to take pride in their work. Be careful of the notes and comments that you make on student work. Be sure that the comments are dignifying and encouraging. Nobody wants to save and repeatedly look at an assignment with negative comments on it.

❏ Add samples regularly but not too often. It is important to get a thorough sample of each step in the writing process, but too many papers and samples can be overwhelming to sort through and organize.

❏ Add a variety of samples documenting each phase of the writing process. Selecting the best example of each stage in the process may give a better picture of what the student is able to do, but including beginning samples of a stage as well as more developed samples can show progress.

❏ Review portfolios frequently. Be sure to include times to look through the portfolios. Giving students suggestions on what to look for as they review their portfolios is an effective way to use the portfolios. Don't just ask students to look through their portfolios. Guide them and point out progress and insights to the writing process. Be their guide as they learn about themselves as writers.

❏ Note the progress of each student. Set up times to meet individually with each student. Acknowledge and praise progress. Be sure to discuss suggestions for each student to improve his or her writing. Be concise. Don't give too many suggestions, as your message may get lost.

❏ Share with parents. Be sure to allow a chance for parents to review their children's portfolios. You may have a homework assignment for students to review their portfolios with parents and have parents write positive comments about student writing and progress.

❏ Have students write a reflection on their writing. Allow time for students to write or dictate reflections about their writing and their writing abilities. These reflections will show progression and growth, as well.

Teacher Checklist of Standards

Name: _____

Skill	First Attempt	Mastery
1. Demonstrates competence in the general skills and strategies of the writing process		
A. Prewriting: Uses prewriting strategies to plan written work		
—discusses ideas with peers		
—draws pictures to generate ideas		
—writes key thoughts and questions		
—rehearses ideas		
—records reactions and observations		
B. Drafting and Revising: Uses strategies to draft and revise written work		
—rereads		
—rearranges words, sentences, and paragraphs to improve or clarify meaning		
—varies sentence types		
—adds descriptive words and details		
—deletes extraneous information		
—incorporates suggestions from peers and teachers		
—sharpens the focus		
C. Editing and Publishing: Uses strategies to edit and publish written work		
—proofreads using a dictionary and other resources		
—edits for grammar, punctuation, capitalization, and spelling at a developmentally appropriate level		
—incorporates illustrations or photos		
—shares finished product		
D. Evaluates own and others' writing		
—asks questions and makes comments about writing		
—helps classmates apply grammatical and mechanical conventions		
E. Dictates or writes with a logical sequence of events (e.g., includes a beginning, middle, & end)		
F. Dictates or writes detailed descriptions of familiar persons, places, objects, or experiences		
G. Writes in response to literature		
H. Writes in a variety of formats (e.g., picture books, letters, stories, poems, information pieces)		

Teacher Checklist of Standards *(cont.)*

Name: _____

Skill	First Attempt	Mastery
2. Demonstrates competence in the stylistic and rhetorical aspects of writing		
A. Uses general, frequently used words to convey basic ideas		
3. Uses grammatical and mechanical conventions in written compositions		
A. Forms letters in print and spaces words and sentences		
B. Uses complete sentences in written compositions		
C. Uses declarative and interrogative sentences in written compositions		
D. Uses nouns in written compositions		
E. Uses verbs in written compositions		
F. Uses adjectives in written compositions		
G. Uses adverbs in written compositions		
H. Uses conventions of spelling in written compositions		
—spells high frequency, commonly misspelled words		
—uses a dictionary and other resources to spell words		
—spells own first and last names		
I. Uses conventions of capitalization in written compositions		
—first and last names		
—first word of a sentence		
J. Uses conventions of punctuation in written compositions		
—uses periods after declarative sentences		
—uses question marks after interrogative sentences		
—uses commas in a series		
4. Gathers and uses information for research purposes		
A. Generates questions about topics of personal interest		
B. Uses books to gather information for research topics		
—uses table of contents		
—examine pictures and charts		

Skill Evaluation

This form is to be used when only specific skills are being assessed in a story. Cut along the dotted line to use this form for more than one student.

Student Name:	Skill:	Skill:	Skill:
Student Name:	Skill:	Skill:	Skill:
Student Name:	Skill:	Skill:	Skill:

Sample Stories

These sample stories are meant to be used as guides only. Students in your class may be above or below the levels of these sample reports. Pull samples from your own class to help you establish standards of competent, emergent, and beginner stories.

Competent

The student provides a centered title. The student begins with an introduction of the character. The story is written logically with a beginning, a middle, and an end. The story contains the story elements of characters, a setting, and a conflict. The student ends the story with a resolution to the conflict. The story is neatly presented and easy to read.

The Missing Bicycle

Once there was a kid detective named Detective Joe. He liked to help the kids in his neighborhood solve mysteries. One day a boy ran in crying. He was very upset. He said someone had stolen his bicycle.

Detective Joe calmed him down. He told him not to worry. He told him he would help. He began asking the boy questions. He wrote down what the boy said in a black book. Detective Joe started looking for clues.

Detective Joe looked all over the neighborhood. He finally found the missing bike. The boy forgot he had left it at his friend's house.

Emergent

This story has a lot of good sentences, but the student needs to work on using capital letters and spelling certain words. The student has a title but needs to center it. This story could use a beginning, a middle, and an end.

the missing bike

detecive joe liked to help kids in the neighborhood. He liked to look for clues and slovee mysteries. He was a good kid. He foudn the bike for the boy. He looked for clues to help him. The boy was so happy they cebecame firneds.

Beginner

The student is learning to write words on the paper for a story. The student needs help with a title, capitalization, punctuation, spelling, and writing complete sentences. The student is using inventive spelling to spell words. There is no logical sequence in this story. This student may still need to dictate the story and rewrite what is written.

boy lost hes bik he wants sum helfo dto finds the bike he thinks That somebudy stole his bike he needs a cop the cop founds his bik

---

Elements
of
Story
Writing

Teaching students the elements of story writing gives them the tools they need to write any number of stories. Once students understand the parts of a story, it is easier for them to write one. This section of story-writing elements will teach students the basic parts of a story. The elements taught in this section are character, setting, conflict, and resolution.

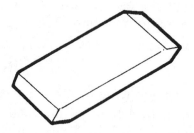

Standards and Benchmarks: 1A, 1F

Characterization

Objective: The students will draw pictures to generate ideas about a character.

Materials

- copy of "Create a Character" (page 26) for each student
- overhead transparency of "Identifying Character Traits" (page 27)
- copy of "Identifying Character Traits" (page 27) for each student
- colored pencils or crayons
- scissors
- copy of *Sylvester and the Magic Pebble* by William Steig (See the bibliography on pages 142 and 143.)

Procedure

1. Read the story aloud to the class. After you have finished, ask students to think about the people in this story. Using the overhead transparency, write the name of a main character from the story in each circle. As a class, brainstorm a list of words that could be used to describe the characters in this story. Write down as many words in the character web as students can generate.

2. Explain to students that these animals are called the characters of this story. The characters are an important part of a story. Characters can be people or animals. Ask students to think back on different stories they have read before. Who were some of the characters in those stories? Encourage students to share examples. (Some examples might include the Berenstain Bears, Clifford, Sesame Street characters, etc.)

3. Next, brainstorm a list of other character traits that can be used to describe a character. Write these on the chalkboard. Then distribute a copy of "Create a Character" (page 26) to each student. Using the list of words on the chalkboard, students select one or more words from the list and create a character. Using colored pencils or crayons, have students draw the face of this character. Some of the descriptions are harder to capture in a drawing than others.

4. Divide students into groups of four or five. Have each student take a turn to share his or her character face. Have students describe to the members in the group all they can about their character. Have students cut out characters and post them on a bulletin board.

Portfolio Piece

Distribute copies of "Identifying Character Traits" (page 27) to students. On this page, have students write down descriptive words about the characters they designed on the character face. Next, have students think of new characters and then write descriptive words for them. Store this page in the students' portfolios. These characters can be used in future stories.

Assessment

- Check to see that students have completed the student pages.
- Check off skills 1A and 1F on the teacher checklist (pages 20 and 21) and use "Elements of Story Writing Assessment Rubric" (page 35) to assess student work.

Create a Character

Sylvester
Character
Traits

Identifying Character Traits

...me of a character in the circle. On each line, write a descriptive
...ls something about the character in the circle. You may add more
... circle if you need them. The first one has been done for you.

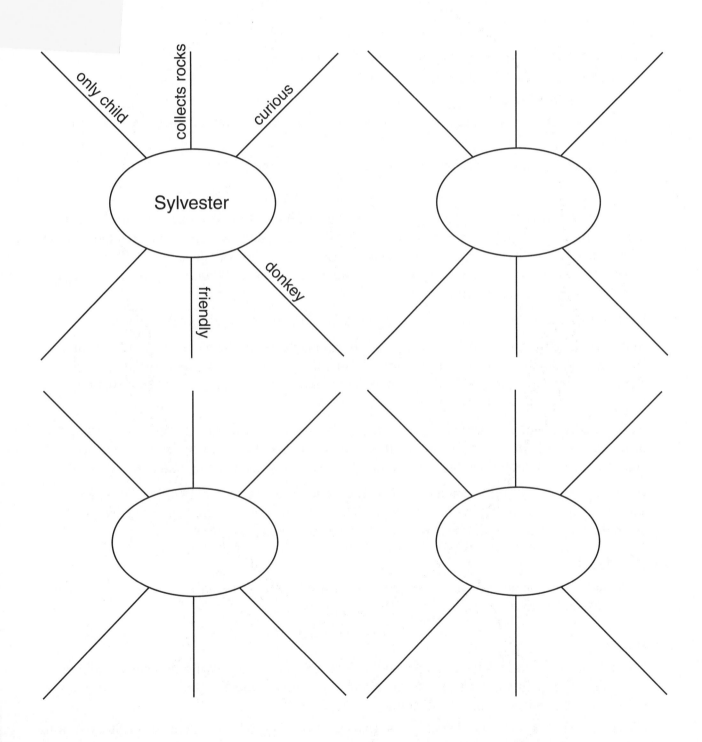

Standards and Benchmarks: 1A

Setting the Stage

Objective: The student will be able to discuss with peers ideas about setting.

Materials

- pictures of scenes (calendar pictures, pictures from magazines, etc.)
- copy of "See a Scene" (page 29) for each student
- crayons or colored pencils
- copy of *Sylvester and the Magic Pebble* by William Steig (See the bibliography on pages 142 and 143.)
- five or six books that you have previously read to your students

Procedure

1. Distribute a copy of "See a Scene" (page 29) to the students. Have students draw a picture of a scene from the book *Sylvester and the Magic Pebble*. After students have completed their scenes, allow them time to share them with the class. Then ask the following questions: *Where does the story take place? How do you know where the story takes place? What are some examples from the story that tell you about its setting?*

2. Explain to students that the setting of a story is where and when the story takes place.

3. Make available to students the cutout pictures from magazines or the pictures from calendars. Have each student select one of the pictures. Using the picture, each student makes up a mini-story about something that took place where the picture shows. Explain to students that the picture is the setting for their mini-story.

4. Divide students into pairs and have them display their pictures and tell the mini-stories using the picture as the settings. Circulate around the room to listen and observe students as they discuss and share ideas about the settings. Ask students to tell you what a setting in a story is.

5. Hold up familiar books that you have read earlier in the year. As you hold up the book, ask students to describe the setting in each book. What are some of the indicators of the setting? What do students remember about where and when the stories take place?

Portfolio Piece

Have each student pick another picture from the pile. Instruct students to place these pictures in their portfolios to use in future stories.

Assessment

- Check to see that students have completed the "See a Scene" page. While students are telling their mini-stories, circulate around the room and ask students what the setting is in a story to see if they have an understanding of the term.
- Check off skill 1A on the teacher checklist (pages 20 and 21) and use "Elements of Story Writing Assessment Rubric" (page 35) to assess student work.

See a Scene

Directions: Draw a scene from the book *Sylvester and the Magic Pebble.*

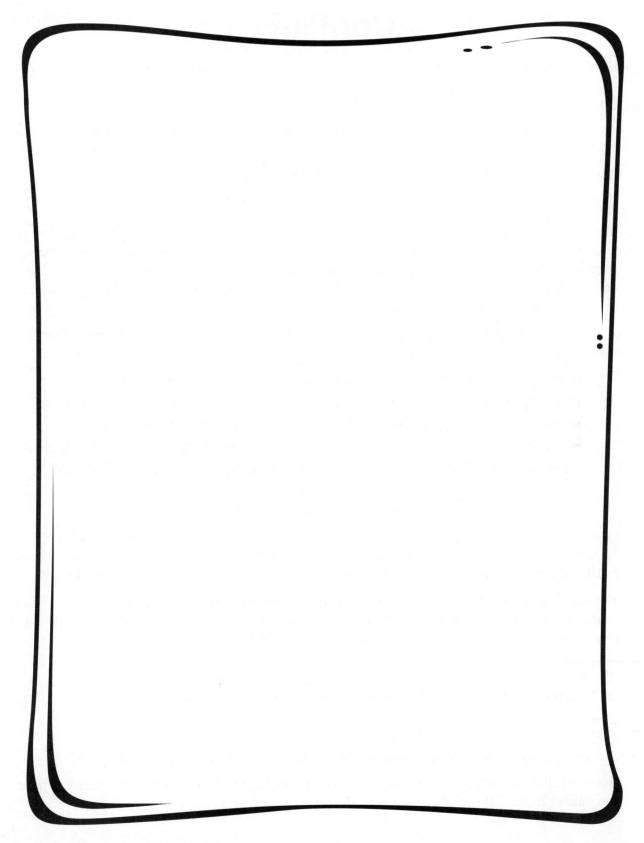

Standards and Benchmarks: 1A

Conflict

Objective: The students will be able to write key thoughts and questions about the conflict in a story.

Materials

- copy of *Sylvester and the Magic Pebble* by William Steig (See the bibliography on pages 142 and 143.)
- copy of "Types of Conflicts" (page 31) for each student

Procedure

1. Reread the story *Sylvester and the Magic Pebble* to your class. Ask students what the problem is in the story. Is there more than one problem? Explain that all stories have a conflict of some sort or another. A conflict can be with nature, society, another person, or with the character himself/herself. Some stories have more than one conflict; some have just one. In *Sylvester and the Magic Pebble*, there are a few conflicts.

2. Divide your class into smaller groups. Give each group a part to dramatize for the rest of the class. The parts to dramatize are as follows:

   - Sylvester wishes that it would stop raining, and he discovers the magic pebble.
   - On the way home, a hungry lion is looking for Sylvester. Sylvester asks to turn into a rock.
   - Sylvester is unable to change back into himself. He is left there day and night.
   - Sylvester's parents are worried and can't find him. Not even the police can find their child.
   - All the dogs in Oatsdale look for Sylvester, but none of them can tell that the rock is Sylvester.
   - Sylvester's parents are miserable, and Sylvester is stuck as a rock this whole time.

3. As students dramatize the parts of the story, have them look for the problems or the conflicts. Discuss the problems or conflicts as a class. List each of the conflicts on the board. Then ask the students if the conflicts are with nature, society, another person, or with the character himself.

4. Distribute copies of "Types of Conflicts" (page 31). Have the students complete this page. When completed, discuss the page as a class. Allow time for students to share problems or conflicts in their own lives and to ask questions to clarify these conflicts.

Portfolio Piece

Place the "Types of Conflicts" page in the students' portfolios to use in future stories.

Assessment

- Check to see that students have completed the "Types of Conflicts" page correctly.
- Check off skill 1A on the teacher checklist (pages 20 and 21) and use "Elements of Story Writing Assessment Rubric" (page 35) to assess student work.

Types of Conflicts

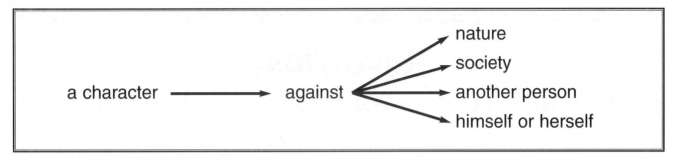

Fill in the chart below using the characters from *Sylvester and the Magic Pebble*. The first one has been done for you. Think of problems or conflicts you have had and write them on the back of this page.

Character or Person	Conflict	Type of Conflict
Sylvester	doesn't like rain	against nature
Sylvester	stuck as pebble	

Standards and Benchmarks: 1A

Resolution

Objective: The students will be able to record reactions to and observations about a resolution in a story.

Materials

- strips of paper (at least one per student)
- bowl
- student portfolios
- book of your choice (See the bibliography on pages 142 and 143.)

Procedure

1. Make strips of paper. On each strip, write a problem or conflict that the students are familiar with, either at home or at school. (Examples may include missing the bus in the morning, running out of your favorite cereal, hurting your best friend's feelings, etc.) Fold these strips of paper in half and place them in a bowl.

2. Ask students how Sylvester's problem of being stuck as a rock was solved. (Sylvester's father found the red pebble and put it on Sylvester's back. When Sylvester said to himself, "I wish I were myself again, I wish I were my real self again," he instantly came back.) Explain to students that this is the resolution. This is how the conflict of not being able to turn back into the donkey by himself was resolved.

3. Hold up the bowl and tell students it is filled with conflicts or problems that need a resolution. One at a time, have each student draw a slip of paper, read aloud the conflict (you may need to help with the reading), and suggest a resolution for the conflict. Continue in this manner until all students have had a turn at resolving a conflict. Then ask the students if there was more than one thing they could have done to solve the conflict. Explain to students that the resolution is a very important part of a story. The resolution usually comes at the end of a story, unless there is more than one conflict in the story. The resolution needs to be believable, and it needs to tie up all the loose ends that are brought up in the story.

4. Now, read a short story of your choice to the class. Before you read, instruct the class to look for the conflict in the story and to observe and record the resolution on a piece of paper. As students turn in these papers, check to see that they have written the correct resolution.

Portfolio Piece

Pull out the "Types of Conflict" (page 31) from the previous lesson. Ask students to write resolutions for the conflicts from their own lives.

Assessment

- Check to see that students have observed and recorded the correct resolution to the story you shared with the class.
- Check off the skill 1A on the teacher checklist (pages 20 and 21) and use "Elements of Story Writing Assessment Rubric" (page 35) to assess student work.

Standards and Benchmarks: 1A

Dissecting a Story

Objective: The students will rehearse ideas with peers in determining the parts of a story.

Materials

- copy of "Parts of a Story" (page 34) for each student
- book of your choice to read to class (See the bibliography on pages 142 and 143.)

Procedure

1. Distribute "Parts of a Story" (page 34) to students. Tell students that they are going to be detectives. As you read a story, they need to listen to get the clues. They are trying to find all the parts of a story from the book you will read. Show them where on the worksheet to write each element of the story. The elements students are looking for are character, setting, conflict, and resolution. Write these words in large letters on the chalkboard. Review what each of these words means so that students have a clear understanding before you begin reading.

2. Read aloud to the class the book you have selected ahead of time. Be sure it is a short story so that it is not too difficult to find the character(s), setting(s), conflict(s), or resolution(s). Read the story slowly so that students have time to write. You may need to read the story more than once.

3. When you have finished reading the story, pair students and have them share what they have written on their papers. Allow time for them to rehearse their ideas about the parts of the story with their partner. Did they get them all answered? Did they come up with the same answers? What was different? Could they find all the characters from the story? What was the conflict? What was the resolution? Students may change their papers, as needed. Circulate around the room to assist students as needed. When students have had time to discuss their thoughts with their partner and to make adjustments, read the story again.

Portfolio Piece

Have students fill in the bottom portion of "Parts of a Story" (page 34). When students have written in all the parts, have them write their stories on separate pieces of paper. Then allow time for students to share their stories aloud with their partners.

Assessment

- Check to see that students have discussed their ideas with a partner and completed the "Parts of a Story" page.
- Check off skill 1A on the teacher checklist (pages 20 and 21) and use "Elements of Story Writing Assessment Rubric" (page 35) to assess student work.

Parts of a Story

Fill in the parts of the story that your teacher will read to you.

Character(s)	
Setting	
Conflict	
Resolution	

Now fill in the parts of your *own* story.

Character(s)	
Setting	
Conflict	
Resolution	

34

Elements of Story Writing
Assessment Rubric

Use the rubric below to assess student progress of the brainstorming standards and benchmarks. The numbers and letters in parentheses correspond with the teacher checklist (pages 20 and 21) in the assessment section.

Competent

- ❏ The student can independently use prewriting strategies to plan written work. (1A)
- ❏ The student can independently discuss ideas with peers.
- ❏ The student can independently draw pictures to generate ideas.
- ❏ The student can independently write key thoughts and questions.
- ❏ The student can independently rehearse ideas.
- ❏ The student can independently record reactions and observations.
- ❏ The student can independently write detailed descriptions of a character, setting, etc. (1F)

Emergent

- ❏ The student can usually use prewriting strategies to plan written work. (1A)
- ❏ The student can usually discuss ideas with peers.
- ❏ The student can usually draw pictures to generate ideas.
- ❏ The student can usually write key thoughts and questions.
- ❏ The student can usually rehearse ideas.
- ❏ The student can usually record reactions and observations.
- ❏ The student can usually write detailed descriptions of a character, setting, etc. (1F)

Beginner

- ❏ The student requires assistance to use prewriting strategies to plan written work. (1A)
- ❏ The student requires assistance to discuss ideas with peers.
- ❏ The student requires assistance to draw pictures to generate ideas.
- ❏ The student requires assistance to write key thoughts and questions.
- ❏ The student requires assistance to rehearse ideas.
- ❏ The student requires assistance to record reactions and observations.
- ❏ The student requires assistance to write detailed descriptions of a character, setting, etc. (1F)

The Writing Process

This section of the unit is meant to teach students how to use the writing process. The writing process will enable students to write a story by brainstorming; drafting; editing; and finally, publishing. This section contains brainstorming webs, story maps, and other graphic organizers which can be used to plan and organize stories. These can be used in a variety of ways. The first way is to incorporate them with lessons. Another way is to use them individually with students. These organizers can assist you in helping a student organize his or her story or brainstorm ideas for a story. The story map can even be used for students who have moved beyond the story outline format in their story writing and are ready for more sophisticated organizers.

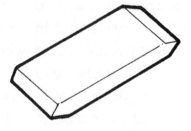

The Writing Process

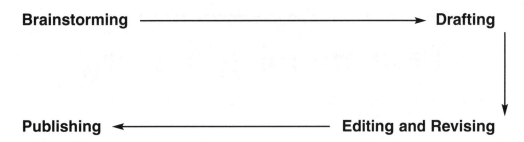

The writing process is the term used to describe the steps a student takes to write a story. Each step of the process is unique, and each step is necessary. Listed below are the main objectives and key points of each step in the writing process.

Brainstorming

The brainstorming step is the beginning stage of the writing process. In this step, the characters are invented, the plot selected, and prior knowledge is tapped into in order to provide a beginning. Brainstorming techniques include things such as webbing, clustering, free writing, and more—whatever it takes to get the ideas down on paper. Brainstorming should be done individually, as well as in groups, as other students' ideas will trigger other ideas and concepts.

Drafting

At this stage in the writing process, students are ready to focus and organize their thoughts and ideas. Assist students in deciding what their stories will be about. What will the characters do? What is the conflict? Where is the setting? Give clear directions and criteria for students to write their drafts. The criteria set up in this unit are that each story needs to have a title, at least six sentences, and a concluding sentence. You may need to alter these criteria to meet the needs and the levels of your students.

Editing and Revising

Now comes the polishing part of the story. At this stage, students look back on what they have written and make corrections in spelling, grammar, punctuation, and capitalization. These are the tools needed by effective writers. Students also need to read their stories and make sure that they make sense and are easy to follow. Are there too many details about the story and characters, or not enough? Are there parts of the story that are missing? What other revisions need to be made for a complete and intriguing story?

Publishing

The last phase of the writing process is the publishing step. At this point, students have brainstormed, drafted, edited, and revised their stories. A nice touch to the final copy is illustrations. Publishing the story can be the most exciting part for students as they share their stories with others. Be sure to plan opportunities for students to present and share their stories with a wide variety of people. This is important, as it will teach the students what an audience likes about a story. Students will be able to tell if they have captured the audience. This can lead to better and better stories being written.

Standards and Benchmarks: 1A, 2A

Brainstorming a Story

Objective: The student will use prewriting strategies to plan a story.

Materials

- copy of "Brainstorming Web" (page 39) for each student
- approximately 20 index cards

Procedure

1. Brainstorming is the beginning stage of the writing process. Getting an idea to write about can be difficult for some children. This first activity will give students a chance to practice brainstorming. Divide your class into groups of four or five students.

2. On about 20 index cards, write one topic (people, places, or things) on each. Give five or more of these cards to each group. The group members place the cards in a pile facedown. Have students draw a card from the pile and brainstorm as many words associated with the topic as they can think of in one minute. For example, if the index card says "dog" on it, then students may write the names of their own pet dogs, types of dogs, colors of dogs, things people can do with dogs, types of dog food, and so forth. After time is up, students share what they wrote with the rest of the group. If students think of something more after listening to other students, they can add it to their list. Continue on in this manner until all of the cards have been used.

3. Ask students about this activity. Some questions you might ask could be: Were there some topics that were harder to come up with words for than others? Did something another student said help you think of something new? Which topic did you have the most words for? Why do you think so?

4. Now, distribute copies of "Brainstorming Web" (page 39) to the students. In the center of the web, students write a topic. This is a topic they want to write a story about. Allow time for students to work independently on this. Then have them get back into their groups. Students take turns sharing their brainstorming webs with the group members. After sharing their webs, they ask for other ideas they can add to their webs.

Portfolio Piece

Students add group members' suggestions to their "Brainstorming Web" pages and place them in their portfolios for future use.

Assessment

- Check to see that students have used the "Brainstorming Web" correctly.
- Check off skill 1A on the teacher checklist (pages 20 and 21) and use "The Writing Process Assessment Rubric" (page 48) to assess student work.

Brainstorming Web

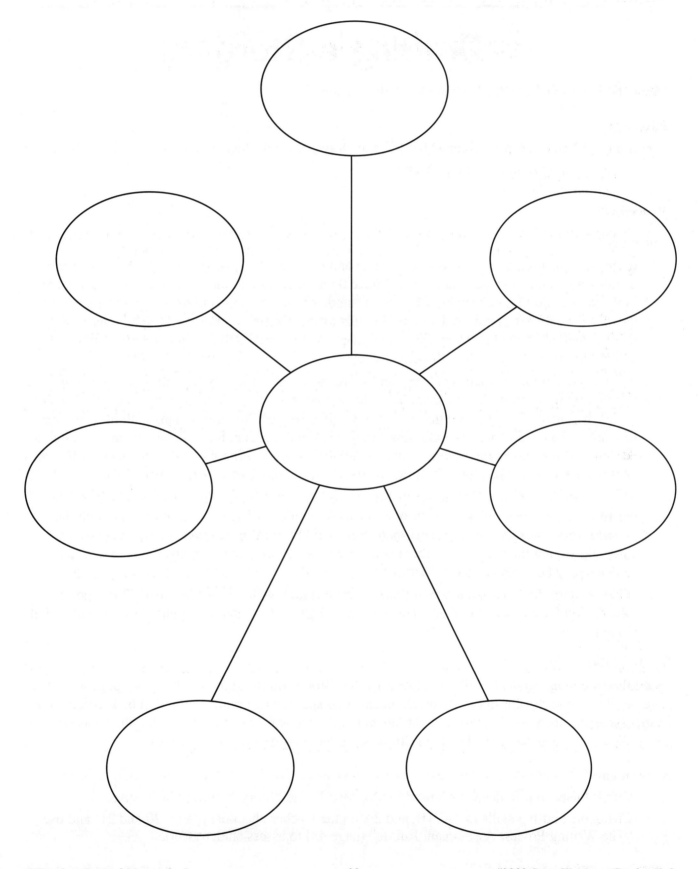

Standards and Benchmarks: 1A, 1B, 2A

Drafting a Story

Objective: The student will use strategies to draft a story.

Materials

- copies of "Story Map I," "Story Map II," and "Story-Writing Plan" (pages 41–43) for each student
- overhead transparency of "Story Map I"
- student portfolios
- maps

Procedure

1. In this lesson, students will learn how to plan and organize the parts of a story. Writing an outline or following a map can help students organize their thoughts and ideas about a story. Show the samples of maps that you have brought. Ask students what a map is used for. Ask students if they have ever used a map. Encourage students to share their experiences. Explain that a story map is used much the same way as a travel map. A story map will lead you from one place to another as you work your way through a story.

2. Ask students to turn to their neighbors and share stories about family trips they have been on. Allow time for each student to share his or her experience. Explain to students that telling a story is easy in person, but when we go to do it in writing, we need to have a plan. Call on volunteers to share personal experiences about times they went to the beach, had a picnic, went camping, or participated in some family outing. As they tell their stories, write down the characters, settings, conflicts, events, and resolutions on the overhead transparency of the story map.

3. Now ask students to think of stories that they want to write about. They may look through their portfolios for brainstorming ideas or other ideas for stories. (They may also look through the Writer's Block box, if needed.) Distribute copies of "Story Map I" (page 41) to students. Circulate around the room to see that the maps are being filled out correctly. (Some of your students may be ready for Story Map II.)

4. When students have completed their maps, demonstrate how to use a story map. Take the information from a map and then write a story, using the story map as a guide. Enlist student help along the way.

Portfolio Piece

Using the story map, students will write drafts of their stories on the story-writing plan (page 43). This page outlines the parts of a story. Remind students that spelling and punctuation will be focused on at a later point in the story-writing process. At this point, the focus needs to be on getting the ideas on paper. When students have finished their drafts, store them in the student portfolios.

Assessment

- Check to see that students have used "Story Map I" and "Story-Writing Plan" correctly.
- Check off drafting skills in 1A, 1B, and 2A on the teacher checklist (pages 20 and 21) and use "The Writing Process Assessment Rubric" (page 48) to assess student work.

Story Map I

Directions: Use this map to record the different parts of your story.

Setting (where and when)

Character(s)

Conflict

Action/Events

Resolution

Story Map II

Directions: Use this map to record the different parts of your story.

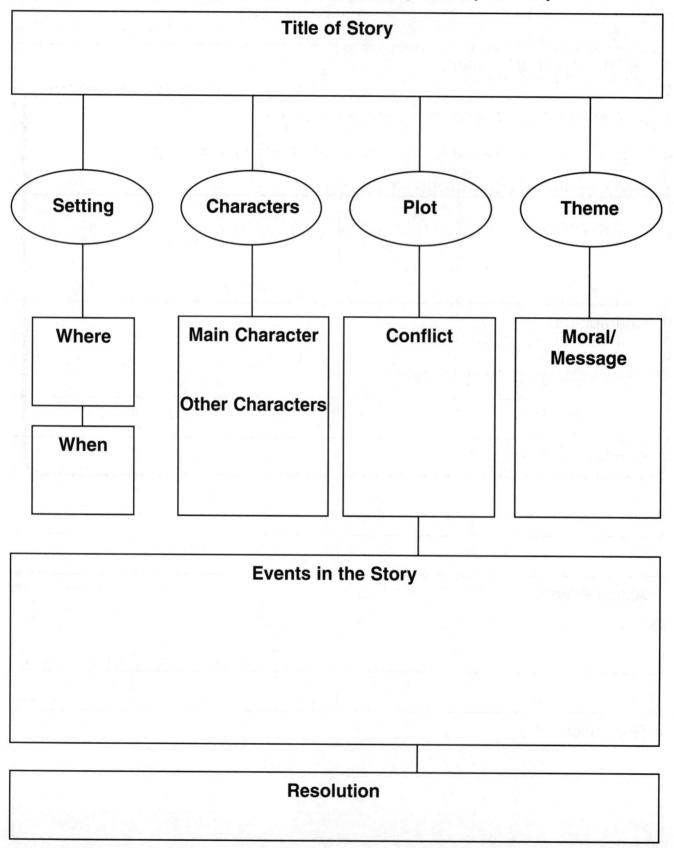

Title of Story

Setting

Characters

Plot

Theme

Where

When

Main Character

Other Characters

Conflict

**Moral/
Message**

Events in the Story

Resolution

Story-Writing Plan

Here is a recipe for writing a story. This story has three paragraphs and has a beginning, a middle, and an end. Write your draft below.

How to Write a Story Beginning

❏ Name the people in the story. (characters)

❏ Tell where and when the story takes place. (setting)

How to Write the Middle of the Story

❏ Write what the characters do.

❏ Tell what happened first.

❏ Write what the problem is. (conflict)

❏ Tell what happened next.

How to Write a Story Ending

❏ Think about the best way things could work out. (resolution)

❏ Finish the story.

_____

_____

_____

_____

_____

_____

_____

_____

Standards and Benchmarks: 1B, 1C, 1D, 3H

Editing and Revising

Objective: The student will use strategies to edit and revise a story.

Materials

- copy of "Proofreading Chart" (page 45) for each student
- overhead transparency of "Proofreading Chart" (page 45)
- student portfolios
- red pens or red pencils

Procedure

1. Students are now ready to edit and revise the stories they drafted in the previous lesson. Explain to the students that it is now time to check their writing for mistakes. This is a very important step in the writing process, and every writer needs to do this every time he or she writes something.

2. Place the overhead transparency of the "Proofreading Chart" (page 45) so that all students can see it. Go through each of the editing marks used to show that mistakes have been made in writing. Go through the sample at the bottom of the page. Highlight the proofreading marks with a red marker.

3. Next, have students pull out their rough drafts from the previous lesson. Distribute a copy of "Proofreading Chart" to each student. Give each student a red pencil or pen. Have the students make editing marks where needed. Then have students exchange papers with partners, and using red pencils or pens, make any editing marks that have been missed on their partners' paper. This is the editing portion of the writing process. Return the stories to their original owners.

4. Now, turn students' attention to the revising process. Have students read their stories again. Have them ask themselves the following questions: (Write these questions on the chalkboard.)
   - Does the story make sense?
   - Does it have a beginning, a middle, and an end?
   - Does the story have a title?
   - Do all the sentences tell about the story?

Portfolio Piece

Allow time for students to make any revisions they need on their papers. Then place the edited rough drafts in the students' portfolios for future use.

Assessment

- Check to see that students have edited their stories correctly.
- Check off editing and revising skills 1B, 1C, 1D, and 3H on the teacher checklist (pages 20 and 21) and use "The Writing Process Assessment Rubric" (page 48) to assess student work.

Proofreading Chart

Use these proofreading marks to show where changes need to be made in story writing.

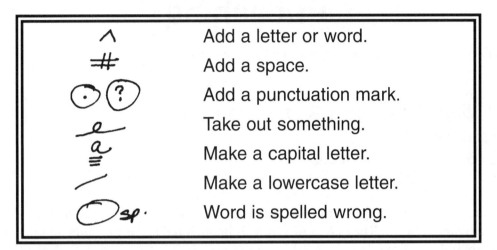

∧	Add a letter or word.
#	Add a space.
⊙ ?	Add a punctuation mark.
ℓ	Take out something.
a̲	Make a capital letter.
/	Make a lowercase letter.
○ sp.	Word is spelled wrong.

Read the story below with the editing marks to see how to use them.

The Big Red Bike

mary could hardly wait to finish her brakefas, it was Saturday and she was going to buy a new bike today. her dad helped her put on her coat and drove to thhe sotre, mary ran in to see the bike she had picked out, but the bike was gone, mary began to cri, where was here bike? marys dad went and talked to the store owneer, he found out that the bike was sold to another girl that morning. mary couldn't believe it, The shop owner told Mary that he could order a new bike.

mary's bike would be here in five days.

Standards and Benchmarks: 1B, 1C, 1D, 3H

Publishing

Objective: The students will use strategies to publish a story.

Materials

- copy of "Story Analysis Scale" (page 47) for each student
- student portfolios
- access to computer for each student

Procedure

1. Students are at the final stage of the writing process. Students have brainstormed, drafted, edited, and revised their stories. They are now ready to publish their stories. Publishing a story can mean many things. Sometimes, publishing will mean writing the edited draft neatly on a clean piece of paper; other times, it may mean typing the story and adding illustrations. For this lesson, students will be typing their stories.

2. Distribute copies of "Story Analysis Scale" to the students. This is for reference only. Show students what you will be looking for when they turn their stories in for grading. Discuss with students that this form will help them make improvements in their writing. Letting students know ahead of time what the expectations are makes it easier for them to meet the goals and expectations. Have students store "Story Analysis Scale" in their portfolios for future reference.

3. Schedule time, if necessary, to use the computers. Spend time demonstrating proper computer use to the students. Determine ahead of time the things you will want your students to do on the computer, and determine what things you will assist them in doing. (For example, you may not want the students to print or save files independently.)

4. Demonstrate how to use a word-processing program. Show students how to center their titles, use the space bar, make indentations, bold letters, and capitalize. It will take some practice for students to become efficient at using the keyboard, so be sure to set aside plenty of time for students to word-process their final drafts. When students are ready to print, ask them to read through their stories on the computer. Some mistakes in the final drafts come from typing errors. Assist students in printing their published stories.

Portfolio Piece

Have students make illustrations to go with the published versions of their stories. Staple the pictures to the typed stories and file them in the student portfolios.

Assessment

- Use the "Story Analysis Scale" to grade student stories. Provide encouraging and supportive feedback for each student regardless of his or her writing level and ability.
- Check off publishing skills 1B, 1C, 1D, and 3H on the teacher checklist (pages 20 and 21) and use "The Writing Process Assessment Rubric" (page 48) to assess student work.

Story Analysis Scale

Student Name: _____

Title of Story:_____

Story Elements	Needs Work	Good	Excellent
The story has . . .			
❏ a title	_____	_____	_____
❏ a good beginning	_____	_____	_____
❏ well-described characters	_____	_____	_____
❏ a setting	_____	_____	_____
❏ a conflict	_____	_____	_____
❏ a resolution.	_____	_____	_____

Editing Skills

	Needs Work	Good	Excellent
The story has . . .			
❏ complete sentences	_____	_____	_____
❏ correct end punctuation	_____	_____	_____
❏ commas used correctly	_____	_____	_____
❏ correct spelling	_____	_____	_____
❏ been written in a logical sequence.	_____	_____	_____

Publishing Skills

	Needs Work	Good	Excellent
The story is . . .			
❏ written or typed neatly	_____	_____	_____
❏ written with capitalized title	_____	_____	_____
❏ illustrated with pictures.	_____	_____	_____

Teacher Comments

Your story is very good in these ways: _____

_____

_____.

Your story could be made better by doing these things: _____

_____

_____.

The Writing Process
Assessment Rubric

Use the rubric below to assess student progress of the brainstorming standards and benchmarks. The numbers and letters in parentheses correspond with the teacher checklist (pages 20 and 21) in the assessment section.

Competent

- ❏ The student can independently use the strategies of the writing process. (1)
- ❏ The student can independently use prewriting strategies to plan a story. (1A)
- ❏ The student can independently use strategies to draft and revise written work. (1B)
- ❏ The student can independently use strategies to edit and publish written work. (1C)
- ❏ The student can independently evaluate his/her own and others' writing. (1D)
- ❏ The student can independently use frequently used words to convey basic ideas. (2A)
- ❏ The student can independently use conventions of spelling in written compositions. (3H)

Emergent

- ❏ The student can usually use the strategies of the writing process. (1)
- ❏ The student can usually use prewriting strategies to plan a story. (1A)
- ❏ The student can usually use strategies to draft and revise written work. (1B)
- ❏ The student can usually use strategies to edit and publish written work. (1C)
- ❏ The student can usually evaluate his/her own and others' writing. (1D)
- ❏ The student can usually use frequently used words to convey basic ideas. (2A)
- ❏ The student can usually use conventions of spelling in written compositions. (3H)

Beginner

- ❏ The student requires assistance to use the strategies of the writing process. (1)
- ❏ The student requires assistance to use prewriting strategies to plan a story. (1A)
- ❏ The student requires assistance to use strategies to draft and revise written work. (1B)
- ❏ The student requires assistance to use strategies to edit and publish written work. (1C)
- ❏ The student requires assistance to evaluate his/her own and others' writing. (1D)
- ❏ The student requires assistance to use frequently used words to convey basic ideas. (2A)
- ❏ The student requires assistance to use conventions of spelling in written compositions. (3H)

Create a Story

With an understanding of story elements, students are now ready to begin drafting a story. Much of this section will be spent teaching students how to write with logic and sequence. Many students at this age are able to get thoughts down on paper, but organizing these thoughts takes time and instruction. Teaching students to write a story with a beginning, a middle, and an ending will enable them to write clearly; and these skills will transfer to other types of writing as well.

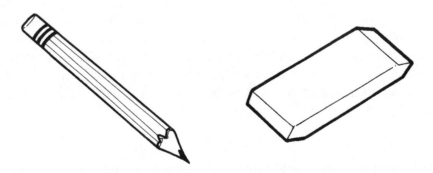

Standards and Benchmarks: 1A, 1B

Where Stories Come From

Objective: The students will incorporate suggestions from peers, teachers, and family members to get ideas for stories.

Materials

- Writer's Block box
- copy of "Story Scavenger Hunt" (page 51) for each student

Procedure

1. Many students have a hard time coming up with an idea for a story to write. This is common, and yet it is a serious problem for some students. Ahead of time, create a Writer's Block box. Fill the box with pictures, miscellaneous items, favorite stories, magazines, etc. Put anything in this box that might help the students come up with ideas for stories. You may even wish to invite students to add to your Writer's Block box.

2. Gather students together and have a discussion about story writing. Explain to them that inside their brains are ideas for millions of stories. Invite students to share the titles of some of their favorite stories. Encourage students to share why they like those stories. Ask them how they think the authors of those stories came up with their ideas.

3. There are a variety of ways that authors come up with ideas. Write these ways on the chalkboard, and discuss the meaning of each of them. Stories come from the world around us and our experiences, interesting objects, other stories we have read or heard, and from ideas or stories in our heads—in other words, our imaginations.

4. Distribute a copy of "Story Scavenger Hunt" (page 51) to the students. Go through the ideas for a story at the top of the page. Then turn students' attention to the bottom part of the paper. This is where students will write down ideas for stories of their own. Give them time to circulate around the room and ask others for ideas. Have them take their papers home and ask family members about story ideas. Students should be recording every idea on the scavenger hunt page. As students share ideas, they may want to write ideas down from another student. This sharing of ideas will help students think, and they will brainstorm even more ideas for stories. Invite students to look through the Writer's Block box for ideas as well.

Portfolio Piece

Place the "Story Scavenger Hunt" page in the students' portfolios to use for future reference. Have students each select one of the story ideas and write a story.

Assessment

- Check to see that students have ideas listed on their "Story Scavenger Hunt" page.
- Check off drafting skills 1A and 1B on the teacher checklist (pages 20 and 21) and use "Create a Story Assessment Rubric" (page 64) to assess student work.

Story Scavenger Hunt

There are many places where stories can be found. Here are a few ideas:

- ❏ Write a different ending or beginning for a favorite story.
- ❏ Write a fairy tale in which your best friend is a character.
- ❏ Write a silly story about a dog and a cat.
- ❏ Write about a place where everything is the color green.
- ❏ Write a story about a teacher who whispered everything.
- ❏ Pretend you are an ice-cream cone.

Now see if you can find some story ideas. Write them below.

- ❏ _____
- ❏ _____
- ❏ _____
- ❏ _____
- ❏ _____
- ❏ _____
- ❏ _____
- ❏ _____

Standards and Benchmarks: 1A, 1B, 1F

Picture a Story

Objective: The students will use details and descriptive words in stories.

Materials

- pictures from magazines or old calendars

- picture of an ocean

- copies of "Brainstorming Web" (page 39) for students

Procedure

1. Distribute a picture to each student. Allow time for them to look at their pictures and talk about what they see. What kinds of stories could they write about the pictures they have? What characters do they visualize in the pictures?

2. Encourage students to use descriptive words to describe their pictures. Give them an example. Hold up a picture of an ocean. Write this sentence on the chalkboard: "This is the ocean." Ask students if they could help you describe the ocean even better. For example, "The ocean is blue and wet." Encourage other descriptive sentences about the ocean. Write down as many descriptive sentences about the ocean as students can create. Explain to them that all of the descriptive ocean sentences help the reader visualize the ocean better than just saying, "This is the ocean." Allow students more time to think of descriptive words to describe their pictures.

3. Distribute copies of "Brainstorming Web" (page 39) and have students write descriptions of their pictures in the center circle. Then allow time for students to describe and write about the pictures on the outside circles of the web.

4. Next, have students write stories about their pictures. Have them use their brainstorming webs that have the descriptive words about their pictures on them. When they have finished, tape all of the pictures on the chalkboard or wall. Then have students come up and read their stories. Class members listen to the stories and see if they can find the pictures that go with the stories. Let the story writers call on students to guess until each right picture has been selected. Continue on until all students have had a turn to read their stories.

Portfolio Piece

Have students write reflections on how well they like their stories. Did they describe their pictures with lots of details? Do the stories go with the pictures? Date the reflections and place them and the stories in the students' portfolios.

Assessment

- Check to see that students have each written a descriptive story about the assigned picture.

- Check off drafting skills 1A, 1B, and 1F on the teacher checklist (pages 20 and 21) and use "Create a Story Assessment Rubric" (page 64) to assess student work.

Standards and Benchmarks: 1A, 1B, 1E

First, Next, Then, Finally

Objective: The students will write a story with a logical sequence of events.

Materials

- comic strips from a local newspaper (at least one for each student)
- scissors
- glue
- 9" x 12" (23 cm x 30 cm) piece of construction paper
- book: *Little Red Riding Hood*

First	Next
Then	Finally

Procedure

1. Read aloud a version of *Little Red Riding Hood* to your class. Give students pieces of paper and have them fold them into fourths. At the top of each square, have students write the words "First," "Next," "Then," and "Finally." These words will help prompt the sequence of the story. Discuss what happens in *Little Red Riding Hood*. Instruct students to fill in each square with what happened in the story of *Little Red Riding Hood*. Have students share their work with the other members of the class.

2. Ahead of time, cut out from a newspaper comic strips that have four or five pictures. You only need the picture parts of the comics and not the words. Blank out the words in the speech bubbles before distributing the comic strips to students. Next, ask students to come up with stories based on the pictures. Have students glue the comic strips to the construction paper. Using the prompts "First," "Next," "Then," and "Finally," have students write stories to go with their comic strips.

3. Give students time to complete and reread their stories. Remind students to look and see if the events of their stories are in order. They may add more events than the comic strip depicts, if desired. Pair students and let them share their comic-strip stories with each other. If there are enough comic strips, allow students to write another story, using the "First, Next, Then, and Finally" method.

Portfolio Piece

Have students color the comic-strip pictures and add more illustrations. Place the story and comic strip in the students' portfolios.

Assessment

- Using the Skill Evaluation (page 22), evaluate students on the skill of being able to write a story with logical sequence. Provide feedback for the student on how well he or she performed that skill.
- Check off drafting skills 1A, 1B, and 1E on the teacher checklist (pages 20 and 21) and use "Create a Story Assessment Rubric" (page 64) to assess student work.

Standards and Benchmarks: 1A, 1B, 1E

Story Sequencing

Objective: The students will rearrange words, sentences, and paragraphs in a story to clarify meaning.

Materials

- copy of "Get It Together!" (page 55) for each student
- copy of children's book to read to the class (See the bibliography on pages 142 and 143.)
- scissors

Procedure

1. Read to the class the children's book you have selected. However, read the story out of order. Read the last page first, then the title page, then a page in the middle, and so forth. Talk with students about how hard it is to understand the story when it is read out of sequence. Explain to students that we need to write our stories in sequence, or in order, so that the reader can understand. Elicit students' responses as to why it is important to read a book in sequence.

2. Now read the story again, but this time, read it in order from start to finish. Distribute a copy of "Get It Together!" (page 55) to each student. This page has a story on it, but the story has been mixed up and is no longer in order. Have students rewrite the story in order so that it is clear and understandable. When finished, allow time for students to read the story with a partner, in the correct order.

3. Have students write another story about Blue, the dog. When they have finished, have students cut up their stories and exchange them with another student. See if students can arrange their partner's story in the correct order.

Portfolio Piece

Using a word-processing program, have students type their stories about Blue, the dog. When they are finished, students color a picture of Blue and file their stories and the pictures of Blue in their portfolios.

Assessment

- Check to see that students have completed "Get It Together!" correctly.
- Check off drafting skills 1A, 1B, and 1E on the teacher checklist (pages 20 and 21) and use "Create a Story Assessment Rubric" (page 64) to assess student work.

Get It Together!

Look at the parts of the story below. All of the parts are mixed up. Rearrange the story so that it is in order. Write the story correctly on the lines below.

Blue looked and looked for his bone.
The Lost Bone
He found the bone under the blanket!
There was a dog named Blue.
He loved to chew on bones.
One day he lost his bone.

_____

_____

_____

_____

_____

_____

_____

_____

_____

_____

_____

_____

_____

Standards and Benchmarks: 1A, 1B, 1E

Story Puzzles

Objective: The students will write a story with a logical sequence of events.

Materials

- copy of "Puzzle Pieces" (page 57) for each student
- scissors
- crayons or colored pencils
- envelope for each student (optional)

Procedure

1. Instruct students that they are to each write a story of their own choice. If students need help with an idea, let them look in the "Writer's Block" box (page 50). They may also use a brainstorming web (page 39) for help.

2. When students have finished their stories, have them reread them for clarity. Many times when students read what they have written, they will find many of their own mistakes in sequence and clarity. Encourage students to read it to themselves, and then pair students with partners to read their stories.

3. Next, distribute copies of "Puzzle Pieces" (page 57). On each square, students are to write a part of their story. There can be more than one sentence in each square, but don't let it get too crowded or hard to read. The title can be one of the squares. If there is room, students may draw a little illustration to depict what is happening during each part of the story. Then have students cut out the squares. Place the squares in envelopes to make it easier to keep track of the puzzle pieces.

4. Pair students with another student. (This can't be the same partner they had previously in this lesson.) The students get together and exchange story puzzles. The student tries to put his/her partner's puzzle pieces in order. When the students have completed the puzzles, have them read through the story puzzles to see if they make sense. When students have completed the puzzles, they ask the owners/writers of the puzzles whether they are correct. Students can make changes or rearrange pieces as needed.

Portfolio Piece

Have students write the stories from their puzzles on paper or type them on a computer. Include illustrations with the stories. Place the stories in the students' portfolios as samples of sequencing.

Assessment

- Use "Story Analysis Scale" (page 47) to evaluate the students' stories.
- Check off drafting skills 1A, 1B, and 1E on the teacher checklist (pages 20 and 21) and use "Create a Story Assessment Rubric" (page 64) to assess student work.

Puzzle Pieces

Directions: Write one part of your story in each of the four squares.

Standards and Benchmarks: 1A, 1B

Story Chains

Objective: The students will use the technique of deleting extraneous information and rearranging words, sentences, and paragraphs to clarify meaning.

Materials

- 1" x 6" (2.5 cm x 15 cm) strips of construction paper (6 or 7 per student)
- 5 or 6 stuffed animals

Procedure

1. Divide your class into groups of four or five. Give each group a stuffed animal. Inform students that they will be writing a story about this stuffed animal. As a group, brainstorm different story lines that can be done with the animal. Students may choose to write about the stuffed animals themselves or about the real animals being represented. Give students plenty of time to discuss.

2. Then have each student begin a story about the animal. Each student should write a title at the top of the page and begin writing a story. After a certain amount of time, have students each pass their papers to the person sitting on their right. The student reads the story and then begins writing where the other student left off. Continue on in this way until the stories come back to their original authors. Inform the last students that they are to write the endings of the stories.

3. Return the stories to the original owners. Have students read the stories. Ask these questions: Is the story easy to understand? Are there parts of the story that need to be taken out? Are there parts that need to be added? Do sentences or words need to be rearranged in order to make sense?

4. Once students have made corrections, they are ready to make a story chain. Have students count the number of sentences (including the title) in the story. They will need that many strips of construction paper. On each strip of paper, students write a sentence from the story. Students staple the strips together to form a chain. The title should be at the top of the chain and the following sentences and conclusion should descend from the top. Hang these chains around the room to demonstrate sequence in stories.

Portfolio Piece

Have students type their story chains on the computer. Students may each select a graphic from the computer to go with their stories. Print stories and place them in the students' portfolios.

Assessment

- Check to see that students have completed story chains about the stuffed animals.
- Check off drafting skills 1A and 1B on the teacher checklist (pages 20 and 21) and use "Create a Story Assessment Rubric" (page 64) to assess student work.

Standards and Benchmarks: 1A, 1B, 1F

Squiggle Writing

Objective: The students will add descriptive words and details to their story writing.

Materials

- copies of "Squiggle Writing Pictures" (page 60) (You will need only one squiggle square per student—some students may have the same squiggle, and that is okay.)
- 8½" x 11" (22 cm x 28 cm) piece of white paper for each student
- markers, crayons, or colored pencils

Procedure

1. Cut out the squiggles on page 60 and distribute one squiggle to each student in the class. Have the students each glue the squiggle to a piece of white paper. Direct students to look at their squiggles. What does each look like? What could be added to the squiggle to finish the picture? Have students use markers, crayons, or colored pencils to finish their pictures.

2. When students have finished their squiggle pictures, divide them into pairs and have them share their squiggle pictures. After sharing their squiggles, students discuss ideas for stories about their squiggle pictures. Each student will be writing a story about his or her squiggle picture.

3. Next, have students brainstorm words that could be used to describe their squiggles. How can they use these words in a story? Give students lined paper and ask them to each draft a story about the squiggle picture. When finished, students reread their squiggle stories, looking for descriptive words about their squiggles.

4. Divide students into groups of four or five. Students will take turns displaying their squiggle pictures and sharing their squiggle stories. Members of each group will be listening for descriptive words about the squiggles. Encourage members of the group to give each student sharing a story feedback on how well that student used descriptive words.

Portfolio Piece

Allow students time to rewrite or type their stories neatly on the computer. Print the finished copies and place them in students' portfolios with their squiggle pictures attached.

Assessment

- Using "Skill Evaluation" (page 22), evaluate students on the skill of being able to use descriptive words to describe the squiggle pictures in their stories. Provide feedback for the students on how well they performed that skill.
- Check off drafting skills 1A and 1B on the teacher checklist (pages 20 and 21) and use "Create a Story Assessment Rubric" (page 64) to assess student work.

Squiggle Writing Pictures

Directions: Cut apart and distribute one squiggle to each student.

Standards and Benchmarks: 1A, 1B, 1E

Mixed-up Stories

Objective: The students will reread and sharpen the focus of a story.

Materials

- copy of "All Mixed Up!" (page 62) for each student

Procedure

1. Begin this lesson by asking different students to provide different parts of a story. For example, ask the first student to briefly describe a character to you. Then ask another student to describe a setting. Ask the next student to give you an example of a conflict. Ask the last student to give you a resolution. Write these four categories on the chalkboard. Using the information that the students gave you, write a short story on the chalkboard. The story might end up silly and the students may laugh, but it is still a story.

2. Distribute a copy of "All Mixed Up!" (page 62) to students. Using this paper, students will select an item from each category to create a story. Circulate around the room as students write their stories to help with instructions, sequence, spelling, or other areas.

3. When finished, students reread their stories to make sure they make sense. Remind students that events, people, and places need to flow together for the reader to understand the story.

Portfolio Piece

Let students each write another mixed-up story to type on the computer. Place the typed versions in the students' portfolios.

Assessment

- Check to see that students have completed "All Mixed Up!" correctly.

- Check off drafting skills 1A, 1B, and 1E on the teacher checklist (pages 20 and 21) and use "Create a Story Assessment Rubric" (page 64) to assess student work.

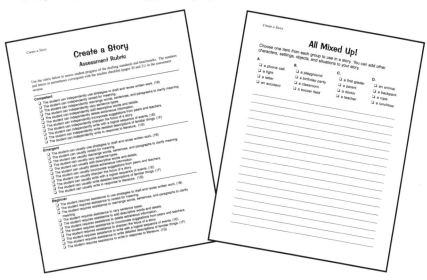

All Mixed Up!

Choose one item from each group to use in a story. You can add other characters, settings, objects, and situations to your story.

A.

❏ a phone call
❏ a fight
❏ a letter
❏ an ac___nt

B.

❏ a playground
❏ a birthday party
❏ a classroom
❏ a soccer field

C.

❏ a first grader
❏ a parent
❏ a doctor
❏ a teacher

D.

❏ an animal
❏ a backpack
❏ a rope
❏ a lunchbox

_____

_____

_____

_____

_____

_____

_____

_____

_____

_____

_____

_____

_____

_____

_____

_____

_____

Standards and Benchmarks: 1A, 1B, 1G, 2A

Change the Story

Objective: The students will write in response to literature.

Materials

- display of familiar stories (e.g., fairy tales and folktales)
- copy of the classic version of *The Three Little Pigs*
- copy of *The True Story of the Three Little Pigs* (See the bibliography on pages 142 and 143.)

Procedure

1. Show students the books that you have on display. Ask students if they are familiar with these stories. Ask students to share their favorites with you. Then ask the students what it would be like to change one of those stories. Select one of the stories to read to the class. Read it to the students. At the end of the reading, ask students to each write a new ending to the story.

2. Allow plenty of time for students to write new endings to the story. Invite students to read their new endings to the class. After students have shared their new endings, ask them what was changed in the new endings. Was it the characters? the resolution to the conflict? the setting? See if you can find examples from your students of each of these changes.

3. Explain to students that many new stories are created by adding or changing something from an already existing story. Read the classic version of *The Three Little Pigs*. Now, read *The True Story of the Three Little Pigs*. Essentially, the story is the same, but this version is told from a different point of view. This story is told from the point of view of the wolf. Ask students how this changes the story. What is different? Share other samples of stories that have been altered in some way. (There are many different versions of the fairy tales and folktales.)

4. Have students each choose a story that they would like to change in some way to make a new story. Have students brainstorm new endings, new beginnings, or other changes. Students then should write their new stories and draw illustrations to go with them.

Portfolio Piece

Let students take turns reading their new versions to another student. Have the listening student make a positive comment about the change that was made. Place these stories in students' portfolios.

Assessment

- Check to see that students have changed stories to create new ones.
- Check off brainstorming skills 1A, 1B, 1G, and 2A on the teacher checklist (pages 20 and 21) and use "Create a Story Assessment Rubric" (page 64) to assess student work.

Create a Story
Assessment Rubric

Use the rubric below to assess student progress of the drafting standards and benchmarks. The numbers and letters in parentheses correspond with the teacher checklist (pages 20 and 21) in the assessment section.

Competent
- ❏ The student can independently use strategies to draft and revise written work. (1B)
- ❏ The student can independently reread for meaning.
- ❏ The student can independently rearrange words, sentences, and paragraphs to clarify meaning.
- ❏ The student can independently vary sentence types.
- ❏ The student can independently add descriptive words and details.
- ❏ The student can independently delete extraneous information.
- ❏ The student can independently incorporate suggestions from peers and teachers.
- ❏ The student can independently sharpen the focus of a story.
- ❏ The student can independently write with a logical sequence of events. (1E)
- ❏ The student can independently write detailed descriptions of familiar things. (1F)
- ❏ The student can independently write in response to literature. (1G)

Emergent
- ❏ The student can usually use strategies to draft and revise written work. (1B)
- ❏ The student can usually reread for meaning.
- ❏ The student can usually rearrange words, sentences, and paragraphs to clarify meaning.
- ❏ The student can usually vary sentence types.
- ❏ The student can usually add descriptive words and details.
- ❏ The student can usually delete extraneous information.
- ❏ The student can usually incorporate suggestions from peers and teachers.
- ❏ The student can usually sharpen the focus of a story.
- ❏ The student can usually write with a logical sequence of events. (1E)
- ❏ The student can usually write detailed descriptions of familiar things. (1F)
- ❏ The student can usually write in response to literature. (1G)

Beginner
- ❏ The student requires assistance to use strategies to draft and revise written work. (1B)
- ❏ The student requires assistance to reread for meaning.
- ❏ The student requires assistance to rearrange words, sentences, and paragraphs to clarify meaning.
- ❏ The student requires assistance to vary sentence types.
- ❏ The student requires assistance to add descriptive words and details.
- ❏ The student requires assistance to delete extraneous information.
- ❏ The student requires assistance to incorporate suggestions from peers and teachers.
- ❏ The student requires assistance to sharpen the focus of a story.
- ❏ The student requires assistance to write with a logical sequence of events. (1E)
- ❏ The student requires assistance to write detailed descriptions of familiar things. (1F)
- ❏ The student requires assistance to write in response to literature. (1G)

Types of Stories

This section of the unit teaches students about some of the different types of stories that they can write. There is a large variety of stories available. There is a listing of story types in the bibliography that you can read to your students for samples. Stories listed in the bibliography are suggestions only. You may use your own story selections as samples, as well.

This section will also introduce peer assessment and formal teacher assessment of stories written by students. Modeling is important for students to understand how to evaluate peers correctly.

When students have finished learning how to write each story type in this section, have students spin the story wheel on page 96 to write the story they spin.

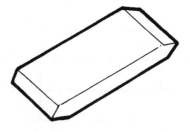

Story-Writing Process Chart

Use the checklist below to keep track of where your students are in the writing process as they complete their stories.

Name of Student	Type of Story	Brainstorm	Draft	Edit/Revise	Publish

Standards and Benchmarks: 1A, 1B, 1C, 1D, 2A

Science Fiction Stories

Objective: The students will be able to write a science fiction story that contains a title, as many sentences as you require*, and a conclusion.

*On the peer and teacher assessment sheets, the number of sentences required will be left blank so that you may determine the criteria which meet the needs of your students.

Materials
- science fiction story (See the bibliography on pages 142 and 143.)
- copies of "Science Fiction Outline," "Science Fiction Peer Assessment," and "Science Fiction Teacher Assessment" (pages 68–70) for each student
- colored pencils or crayons

Prewriting
1. Read a science fiction story to your class. Ask students what a science fiction story is. What are the things that make it a science fiction story? Science fiction is a story based on science where life as we know it has been dramatically changed. Sometimes it is the characters that have been altered (aliens, dinosaurs, etc.), or the setting (outer space, earth with different surroundings, the moon, etc.).
2. Brainstorm with your class a list of things that if scientifically changed would alter the way we live our lives. (What if our clocks stopped working? or everyone's skin turned green? or the sun stayed up night and day? etc.) Make a list of these changes on the chalkboard. Have each student select one change to write a science fiction story about.

Drafting
1. Distribute copies of "Science Fiction Outline" (page 68) to students. Have students answer the questions to prepare for writing their science fiction stories.
2. When students have finished the worksheet, have them write the drafts of their science fiction stories. Go over the criteria for the science fiction story (see objective above). Clarify with students the expectations for these stories.

Editing and Revising
1. When the stories are drafted, pair students up with a partner, and have students read each others' stories. Provide "Science Fiction Peer Assessment" for this purpose. Partners should check to make sure that all the criteria for the science fiction story have been met.
2. Following the peer editing, students should make any necessary changes and revisions before writing the final copies of the stories.

Publishing and Assessment
1. Students should type their drafts, using a word-processing program on the computer. Students could illustrate their final copies with a picture of a character or the scenery.
2. Use "Science Fiction Teacher Assessment" (page 70) to evaluate the final copies of the science fiction stories.

Science Fiction Outline

Answer these questions to help organize your story.

1. Who was involved in the story? (Describe the characters. What do they look like? What can they do?)_____

   _____

   _____

2. Where did it take place? _____

   _____

   _____

3. What does it look like? Is it hot or cold?_____

   _____

   _____

4. What happened to the world? _____

   _____

   _____

5. What has been changed about the world? _____

   _____

   _____

6. What happened in the story?_____

   _____

   _____

7. How did it end? _____

   _____

   _____

8. What is the title of the story?_____

   _____

   _____

Science Fiction

Peer Assessment

Author's Name: _____

Title of Story:_____

Editor's Name:_____

Editor

Did the author write a science fiction story that . . .

❑ changed something about the world?

❑ had a title?

❑ had at least _____ sentences?

❑ had a conclusion?

Author

Before you write your final copy, did you remember to . . .

❑ make any changes that your editor suggested?

❑ check for correct spelling?

❑ check for correct punctuation?

❑ check for correct capitalization?

Complete the following sentences.

1. My favorite part of my story is when _____

_____

_____

_____

2. I need help on _____

_____

_____

_____

Science Fiction
Teacher Assessment

Author's Name: _____

Title of Story:_____

Did the author write a science fiction story that . . .

❑ changed something about the world?

❑ had a title?

❑ had at least_____sentences?

❑ had a conclusion?

Did the student . . .

❑ write or type the story neatly?

❑ use correct spelling?

❑ use correct punctuation?

❑ use correct capitalization?

Feedback from the teacher:

1. Your story is strong in these ways: _____

   _____

   _____

   _____

2. You could make your story better by doing the following: _____

   _____

   _____

   _____

Standards and Benchmarks: 1A, 1B, 1C, 1D, 2A

Personal Narrative Stories

Objective: The students will be able to write a personal narrative that includes an event from his or her life, contains a title, as many sentences as you require*, and a conclusion.

*On the peer and teacher assessment sheets, the number of sentences required will be left blank so that you may determine the criteria which meet the needs of your students.

Materials

- copies of "Personal Inventory," "Personal Narrative Peer Assessment," and "Personal Narrative Teacher Assessment" (pages 72–74) for each student
- colored pencils or crayons
- piece of black construction paper for each student
- scissors

Prewriting

1. Ahead of time, write on the chalkboard at least two paragraphs about a personal story or event from your life. Be sure to include a title and have a conclusion to the story. Students will love to hear about when you were young. Share the personal story with the class and answer any questions that the students may have.

2. Ask students to share examples from their own lives with the class. If there are a lot of students that would like to share, have them turn to the student sitting next to them and share a story with each other. That way all students have a chance to share, and you can get students back on task.

Drafting

1. Distribute copies of "Personal Inventory" (page 72) to students. Have students answer the questions to prepare for writing their personal stories.

2. When students have finished the worksheet, have them each select a topic and write the drafts of their personal stories. Go over the criteria for the personal story (see objective above). Clarify with students the expectations for these stories.

Editing and Revising

1. When the stories are drafted, pair students and have them read each others' stories. Provide the "Personal Narrative Peer Assessment" for this purpose. Partners should check to make sure that all the criteria for the personal narrative story have been met.

2. Following the peer editing, students should make any necessary changes and revisions before writing the final copies of the stories.

Publishing and Assessment

1. Students should type their drafts, using a word-processing program. Using black paper, make a silhouette of each student to go with the published personal story. (A silhouette can be made by putting the child in front of an overhead projector so that the outline of his or her head shows on the wall. Tape the black paper to the wall. Trace and cut out the silhouette of the child's head.)

2. Use "Personal Narrative Teacher Assessment" (page 74) to evaluate the final copies of the personal narrative stories.

Personal Inventory

Answer these questions to help get ideas for your personal story.

1. Where were you born?

   _____

2. What are some things that you are good at?

   _____

3. What do you like to do with your family?

   _____

4. What teachers have you had?

   _____

5. What do you remember about holidays (Christmas, Thanksgiving, etc.)?

   _____

6. What are some activities you have done with your family?

   _____

7. Who are your friends? What are some activities that you have done with your friends?

   _____

8. What do you remember about school?

   _____

9. What are some of your nicknames? How did you get your nicknames?

   _____

10. What are some funny stories about you?

   _____

   _____

   _____

   _____

   _____

Personal Narrative
Peer Assessment

Author's Name: _____

Title of Story:_____

Editor's Name:_____

Editor

Did the author write a personal narrative that . . .

- ❑ shared an event from his or her life?
- ❑ had a title?
- ❑ had at least _____ sentences?
- ❑ had a conclusion?

Author

Before you write your final copy, did you remember to . . .

- ❑ make any changes that your editor suggested?
- ❑ check for correct spelling?
- ❑ check for correct punctuation?
- ❑ check for correct capitalization?

Complete the following sentences.

1. The favorite part of my story is when _____

   _____

   _____

2. I need help on _____

   _____

   _____

   _____

Personal Narrative

Teacher Assessment

Author's Name: _____

Title of Story:_____

Did the author write a personal story that . . .

❑ shared an event from his or her life?

❑ had a title?

❑ had at least _____ sentences?

❑ had a conclusion?

Did the student . . .

❑ write or type the story neatly?

❑ use correct spelling?

❑ use correct punctuation?

❑ use correct capitalization?

Feedback from the teacher:

1. Your story is strong in these ways: _____

   _____

   _____

   _____

2. You could make your story better by doing the following: _____

   _____

   _____

   _____

Standards and Benchmarks: 1A, 1B, 1C, 1D, 2A

Mystery Stories

Objective: The students will be able to write a mystery story that contains a title, as many sentences as you require*, and a conclusion.

*On the peer and teacher assessment sheets, the number of sentences required will be left blank so that you may determine the criteria which meet the needs of your students.

Materials

- mystery story (See the bibliography on pages 142 and 143.)
- copies of "Mystery Story Peer Assessment" and "Mystery Story Teacher Assessment" (pages 76 and 77) for each student
- colored pencils or crayons

Prewriting

1. Read a mystery story to your class. Determine what is needed in a mystery story. (There is a mystery, someone looking to solve the mystery, and a resolution.)
2. Pretend that a student in your class is missing his/her lunch money. Ask your class how they would solve the mystery of the missing lunch money. What would they do? Who could they ask? (Examples could include these: Ask students in class if they have found money, teacher could ask for any witnesses that saw children playing with money, etc.) Make a list of ideas that students have to solve the mystery.

Drafting

1. Explain to students that they have just written an outline for a mystery story. First, they need to say what the mystery is; and then, one by one, students share in their stories the processes they went through in order to solve the mysteries.
2. Go over the criteria for the mystery story (see objective above). Clarify with students the expectations for these stories. Allow time for students to draft their mystery stories.

Editing and Revising

1. When the stories are drafted, pair students up with a partner and have students read each others' stories. Provide copies of "Mystery Story Peer Assessment" (page 76) for this purpose. Partners should check to make sure that all the criteria for the mystery story have been met.
2. Following the peer editing, students should make any necessary changes and revisions before writing the final copies of the stories.

Publishing and Assessment

1. Students should type their drafts, using a word-processing program on the computer. Students can illustrate their final copies with a picture of a character or the scenery.
2. Use "Mystery Story Teacher Assessment" (page 77) to evaluate the final copies of mystery stories.

Mystery Story
Peer Assessment

Author's Name: _____

Title of Story:_____

Editor's Name:_____

Editor

Did the author write a story that . . .

❏ solved a mystery?

❏ had a title?

❏ had at least _____ sentences?

❏ had a conclusion?

Author

Before you write your final copy, did you remember to . . .

❏ make any changes that your editor suggested?

❏ check for correct spelling?

❏ check for correct punctuation?

❏ check for correct capitalization?

Complete the following sentences.

1. My favorite part of my story is when _____

_____

_____

2. I need help on _____

_____

_____

Mystery Story
Teacher Assessment

Author's Name: _____

Title of Story:_____

Did the author write a story that . . .

❏ solved a mystery?

❏ had a title?

❏ had at least _____ sentences?

❏ had a conclusion?

Did the author . . .

❏ write or type the story neatly?

❏ use correct spelling?

❏ use correct punctuation?

❏ use correct capitalization?

Feedback from the teacher:

1. Your story is strong in these ways: _____

_____

_____

_____

2. You could make your story better by doing the following: _____

_____

_____

_____

Standards and Benchmarks: 1A, 1B, 1C, 1D, 2A

Fantasy Stories

Objective: The students will be able to write a fantasy story that contains a title, as many sentences as you require*, and a conclusion.

*On the peer and teacher assessment sheets, the number of sentences required will be left blank so that you may determine the criteria which meet the needs of your students.

Materials

- fantasy story (See the bibliography on pages 142 and 143.)
- copies of "A Day in the Life of . . . ," "Fantasy Story Peer Assessment," and "Fantasy Story Teacher Assessment" (pages 79–81) for each student

Prewriting

1. Read a fantasy story to your class. (See suggestions in the bibliography on pages 142 and 143.) Discuss the elements of a fantasy story. (Fantasy stories are not based on reality. There are usually people, places, or things in a fantasy that have powers or act in ways that do not fit the rules of reality. Some other examples of fantasy stories are many of the fairy tales.) What were the things in the story you read that made it a fantasy?

2. Go through a list of fairy tales and see if students can pinpoint which people, animals, or parts of the story do things that make the story a fantasy.

Drafting

1. Distribute a copy of "A Day in the Life of . . ." (page 79) to each student. Have students pretend they are an item in the classroom (such as an eraser, a pencil, a clock, etc.) and tell a story about what happens to them.

2. Go over the criteria for the fantasy story (see objective above). Clarify with students the expectations for these stories. Allow time for students to draft their fantasy stories.

Editing and Revising

1. When the stories are drafted, pair students and have them read each others' stories. Provide "Fantasy Story Peer Assessment" (page 80) for this purpose. Partners should check to make sure that all the criteria for the fantasy story have been met.

2. Following the peer editing, students should make any necessary changes and revisions before writing the final copies of the stories.

Publishing and Assessment

1. Students should type their drafts, using a word-processing program on the computer. Students could illustrate their final copies with a picture of a character or the scenery.

2. Use "Fantasy Story Teacher Assessment" (page 81) to evaluate the final copies of the fantasy stories.

A Day in the Life of . . .

Fantasy Story
Peer Assessment

Author's Name: _____

Title of Story:_____

Editor's Name:_____

Editor

Did the author write a story that . . .

❑ had a fantasy—something that could only happen in someone's imagination—in it?

❑ had a title?

❑ had at least _____ sentences?

❑ had a conclusion?

Author

Before you write your final copy, did you remember to . . .

❑ make any changes that your editor suggested?

❑ check for correct spelling?

❑ check for correct punctuation?

❑ check for correct capitalization?

Complete the following sentences.

1. My favorite part of my story is when _____

_____

_____

2. I need help on _____

_____

_____

80

Fantasy Story
Teacher Assessment

Author's Name: _____ .

Title of Story:_____

Did the author write a story that . . .

❏ had a fantasy—something that could only happen in someone's imagination—in it?

❏ had a title?

❏ had at least _____ sentences?

❏ had a conclusion?

Did the student . . .

❏ write or type the story neatly?

❏ use correct spelling?

❏ use correct punctuation?

❏ use correct capitalization?

Feedback from the teacher:

1. Your story is strong in these ways: _____

_____

_____

_____

2. You could make your story better by doing the following:

_____

_____

_____

_____

Standards and Benchmarks: 1A, 1B, 1C, 1D, 2A

Myths

Objective: The students will be able to write a myth that contains a title, as many sentences as you require*, and a conclusion.

*On the peer and teacher assessment sheets, the number of sentences required will be left blank so that you may determine the criteria which meet the needs of your students.

Materials

- myth (See the bibliography on pages 142 and 143.)
- copies of "Myths Peer Assessment" and "Myths Teacher Assessment" (pages 83 and 84) for each student
- crayons or colored pencils

Prewriting

1. Begin by explaining to your students that a myth is a story that explains why something is so. It is not a true story but is a story that gives a logical explanation. Read a myth to your class. What is the myth in this story? Is it true? Myths usually provide an explanation for why something is so in nature.

2. As a class, brainstorm a list of myths, or explanations, that students could write stories about. (Some examples might include these: Why do bees sting? Why does the moon go down? Why does a tree drop its leaves? Why does a flower smell pretty? Why does the thunder come after lightning?)

Drafting

1. Go over the criteria for the myth (see objective above). Clarify with students the expectations for these stories. Allow time for students to draft their myths.

Editing and Revising

1. When the story is drafted, pair students and have them read each others' stories. Provide copies of "Myths Peer Assessment" (page 83) for this purpose. Partners should check to make sure that all the criteria for the myth have been met.

2. Following the peer editing, students should make any necessary changes and revisions before writing the final copies of their stories.

Publishing and Assessment

1. Students should type their drafts, using a word-processing program on the computer. Students could illustrate their final copies with a picture of a character or the scenery.

2. Use "Myths Teacher Assessment" (page 84) to evaluate the final copies of the myths.

Myths
Peer Assessment

Author's Name: _____

Title of Story:_____

Editor's Name:_____

Editor

Did the author write a myth that . . .

❑ explained why something is so?

❑ had a title?

❑ had at least _____ sentences?

❑ had a conclusion?

Author

Before you write your final copy, did you remember to . . .

❑ make any changes that your editor suggested?

❑ check for correct spelling?

❑ check for correct punctuation?

❑ check for correct capitalization?

Complete the following sentences.

1. My favorite part of my story is when _____

_____

_____

2. I need help on _____

_____

_____

Myths
Teacher Assessment

Author's Name: _____

Title of Story: _____

Did the author write a myth that . . .

❏ explained why something is so?

❏ had a title?

❏ had at least _____ sentences?

❏ had a conclusion?

Did the author . . .

❏ write or type the story neatly?

❏ use correct spelling?

❏ use correct punctuation?

❏ use correct capitalization?

Feedback from the teacher:

1. Your myth is strong in these ways: _____

_____

_____

_____

_____

2. You could make your myth better by doing the following: _____

_____

_____

Standards and Benchmarks: 1A, 1B, 1C, 1D, 2A

Fables

Objective: The students will be able to write a fable that contains a title, as many sentences as you require*, and a conclusion.

*On the peer and teacher assessment sheets, the number of sentences required will be left blank so that you may determine the criteria which meet the needs of your students.

Materials

- fable (See the Web page address below.)
- copy of "Fables Peer Assessment" and "Fables Teacher Assessment" (pages 86 and 87) for each student

Preparation

Look up the following Web page: *http://www.pacificnet.net/~johnr/aesop/*. This Web page has many fables that can be downloaded and printed for use in your classroom. It also has lesson plans that you could use to develop fable writing in your class.

Prewriting

1. Read a fable to your class. Discuss the elements of a fable. (A fable is a story that makes a point, teaches, or advises. A fable has a moral at the end of the story.) Use the *Aesop's Fables* Web page for examples of fables.
2. Have students think about actual incidents that they have heard or read about which they feel teach something.

Drafting

Go over the criteria for a fable (see objective above). Clarify with students the expectations for these stories. Allow time for students to draft their fables.

Editing and Revising

1. When the stories are drafted, pair students and have them read each others' stories. Provide copies of "Fables Peer Assessment" (page 86) for this purpose. Partners should check to make sure that all the criteria for the fable have been met.
2. Following the peer editing, students should make any necessary changes and revisions before writing the final copies of their stories.

Publishing and Assessment

1. Students should type their drafts, using a word-processing program on the computer. Students could illustrate their final copies with a picture of a character or the scenery.
2. Use "Fables Teacher Assessment" (page 87) to evaluate the final copies of the fables.

Fables

Peer Assessment

Author's Name: _____

Title of Story: _____

Editor's Name: _____

Editor

Did the author write a fable that . . .

❏ made a point or taught something?

❏ had a title?

❏ had at least _____ sentences?

❏ had a conclusion?

Author

Before you write your final copy, did you remember to . . .

❏ make any changes that your editor suggested?

❏ check for correct spelling?

❏ check for correct punctuation?

❏ check for correct capitalization?

Complete the following sentences.

1. My favorite part of my story is when _____

   _____

   _____

2. I need help on _____

   _____

   _____

Fables

Teacher Assessment

Author's Name: _____

Title of Story: _____

Did the author write a fable that . . .

❏ made a point or taught something?

❏ had a title?

❏ had at least _____ sentences?

❏ had a conclusion?

Did the student . . .

❏ write or type the story neatly?

❏ use correct spelling?

❏ use correct punctuation?

❏ use correct capitalization?

Feedback from the teacher:

1. Your fable is strong in these ways:_____

   _____

   _____

   _____

2. You could make your fable better by doing the following: _____

   _____

   _____

   _____

Standards and Benchmarks: 1A, 1B, 1C, 1D, 2A

Comedic Stories

Objective: The student will be able to write a comedy that contains a title, as many sentences as you require*, and a conclusion.

*On the peer and teachers assessment sheets, the number of sentences required will be left blank so that you may determine the criteria which meet the needs of your students.

Materials

- comedic story (See the bibliography on pages 142 and 143.)
- copy of "Comedic Story Peer Assessment" and "Comedic Story Teacher Assessment" (pages 90 and 91) for each student

Prewriting

1. Read a comedy to your class. Discuss the elements of a comedy with your students. (A comedy is meant to make the reader laugh.) Were there things in this story that were funny?

2. As a class, brainstorm a list of events or occurrences that are funny (for example: slipping on a banana peel, a dog dressed up like a clown, a teacher who forgets her name, etc.). There are things in everyday life that are funny. Allow time for students to talk with a student next to them about things that are funny. Share the suggestions and ideas as a class.

Drafting

1. Distribute a copy of "Writing a Comedy" (page 89) to each student. Have students select a funny event that they want to incorporate into their comedy. Using the "Writing a Comedy" page, students are to write out a story plan for their comedy.

2. Go over the criteria for the comedic story (see objective above). Clarify with students the expectations for these stories. Allow time for students to draft their comedic stories.

Editing and Revising

1. When the stories are drafted, pair students and have them read each others' stories. Provide copies of "Comedic Story Peer Assessment" (page 90) for this purpose. Partners should check to make sure that all the criteria for the comedic story have been met.

2. Following the peer editing, students should make any necessary changes and revisions before writing the final copies of their stories.

Publishing and Assessment

1. Students should type their drafts, using a word-processing program on the computer. Students could illustrate cartoons to go with their funny stories.

2. Use "Comedic Story Teacher Assessment" (page 91) to evaluate the final copies of the comedic stories.

Writing a Comedy

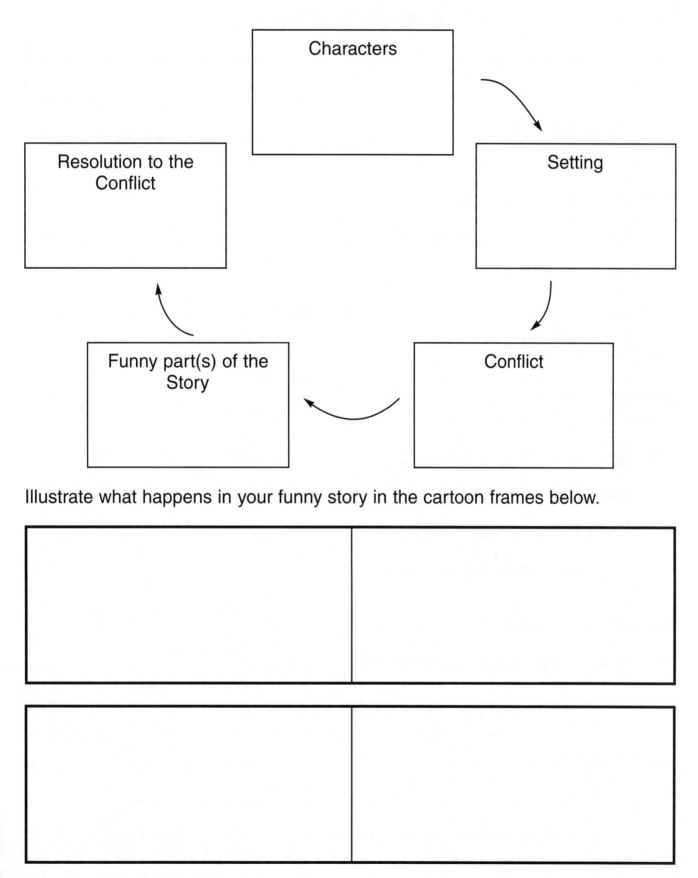

Illustrate what happens in your funny story in the cartoon frames below.

Comedic Story

Peer Assessment

Author's Name: _____

Title of Story: _____

Editor's Name: _____

Editor

Did the author write a story that . . .

- ❏ was funny and entertaining?

- ❏ had a title?

- ❏ had at least _____ sentences?

- ❏ had a conclusion?

Author

Before you write your final copy, did you remember to . . .

- ❏ make any changes that your editor suggested?

- ❏ check for correct spelling?

- ❏ check for correct punctuation?

- ❏ check for correct capitalization?

Complete the following sentences.

1. My favorite part of my story is when _____

   _____

   _____

2. I need help on _____

   _____

   _____

Comedic Story
Teacher Assessment

Author's Name: _____

Title of Story: _____

Did the author write a story that . . .

❏ was funny and entertaining?

❏ had a title?

❏ had at least _____ sentences?

❏ had a conclusion?

Did the author . . .

❏ write or type the story neatly?

❏ use correct spelling?

❏ use correct punctuation?

❏ use correct capitalization?

Feedback from the teacher:

1. Your story is strong in these ways: _____

_____

_____

_____

2. You could make your comedic story better by doing the following: _____

_____

_____

_____

_____

Standards and Benchmarks: 1A, 1B, 1C, 1D, 2A

Adventure Stories

Objective: The students will be able to write an adventure story that contains a title, as many sentences as you require*, and a conclusion.

*On the peer and teacher assessment sheets, the number of sentences required will be left blank so that you may determine the criteria which meet the needs of your students.

Materials

- adventure story (See the bibliography on pages 142 and 143.)
- copy of "Adventure Story Starters," "Adventure Story Peer Assessment," and "Adventure Story Teacher Assessment" (pages 93–95) for each student

Prewriting

1. Read an adventure story to your class.
2. Discuss the elements of an adventure story. (Adventure stories have some sort of adventure in them. Some examples of adventure might include climbing a big mountain, going to the first day of school, learning to ride a bike, going to the principal's office, etc. Remember the things that a first and second grader would consider an adventure will be different from those of an adult.) Ask the students the following question: What was the adventure in the book we just read?

Drafting

1. Distribute a copy of "Adventure Story Starters" (page 93) to each student. Have students select one of the story starters and finish the story by telling what happens in the adventure.
2. Go over the criteria for an adventure story (see objective above). Clarify with students the expectations for these stories. Allow time for students to draft their adventure stories.

Editing and Revising

1. When the stories are drafted, pair students and have them read each others' stories. Provide copies of "Adventure Story Peer Assessment" (page 94) for this purpose. Partners should check to make sure that all the criteria for the adventure story have been met.
2. Following the peer editing, students should make any necessary changes and revisions before writing the final copies of their stories.

Publishing and Assessment

1. Students should type their drafts, using a word-processing program on the computer. Students could illustrate their final copies with a picture of a character or the scenery.
2. Use "Adventure Story Teacher Assessment" (page 95) to evaluate the final copies of the adventure stories.

Adventure Story Starters

Story #1

Sam shouted loudly so that I could hear. He yelled that he thought I was a chicken for not wanting to go into the haunted house. Sam went on in and began climbing up the broken staircase. I came to the doorway and said I thought the stairs were going to break. Sam just said I was afraid of stairs, ghosts, and haunted houses. Then Karen came up and tried to get me to go in. She said that she would go with me, and that way Sam wouldn't think I was a chicken. I decided not to go in. Karen went on in to follow Sam. I sat and waited for over half an hour. Suddenly . . .

Story #2

The noontime blast of the firehouse siren announced the start of the town's bike race. For months, Meg had been practicing. She wanted to win first prize. The first place winner got a brand new ten-speed bike. At first, the hours of practice seemed to pay off as she sped ahead of all the other bikers. Then, from out of nowhere, George whizzed past. There were only a few laps to go . . .

Story #3

Martha and Kathryn had been hiking all day in the woods. Now they were miles from nowhere. The sun was starting to set, and Martha suggested that they head back. Kathryn agreed that it was a good idea. The girls looked around for some trail markers. They couldn't find any. "Oh, no!" said Martha, "We're lost! And we don't even have a flashlight!"

Story #4

Kristen ran into the stable and threw her arms around Ginger. Ginger was Kristen's very own horse. "They can't sell you," sobbed Kristen. She clung to Ginger's mane and stroked it gently. She cried over and over again. All of a sudden, she jumped on Ginger's back and they raced out of the stable.

Story #5

Emily jumped out of bed and quickly put on her robe. She ran down the stairs in such a hurry! Was she going to be late on the first day of school? She was so nervous about going into second grade. She had heard that mean Mary was going to be in her class. She was scared of her. Emily ate her breakfast and ran up to get dressed. Just then the phone rang. Emily could hear her mom talking on the phone. She was talking to Mrs. Marsh, her teacher! What could this mean? Emily's mom yelled, "Emily, it's for you!"

Story #6

The snake came slithering out of its cage. Not one of the students in Mr. Schmidt's class even noticed. Soon after the snake slithered off the counter, the lunch bell rang. All of the students ran to get their lunches and then lined up at the door. When the bell rang again for the students to come back from recess, they opened the door. Anne was the first one back to her seat. Suddenly, she screamed.

Adventure Story
Peer Assessment

Author's Name: _____

Title of Story: _____

Editor's Name: _____

Editor

Did the author write a story that . . .

❑ had an adventure in it?

❑ had a title?

❑ had at least _____ sentences?

❑ had a conclusion?

Author

Before you write your final copy, did you remember to . . .

❑ make any changes that your editor suggested?

❑ check for correct spelling?

❑ check for correct punctuation?

❑ check for correct capitalization?

Complete the following sentences.

1. My favorite part of my story is when _____

_____

_____

2. I need help on _____

_____

_____

Adventure Story

Teacher Assessment

Author's Name: _____

Title of Story: _____

Did the author write a story that . . .

❏ had an adventure in it?

❏ had a title?

❏ had at least _____ sentences?

❏ had a conclusion?

Did the author . . .

❏ write or type the story neatly?

❏ use correct spelling?

❏ use correct punctuation?

❏ use correct capitalization?

Feedback from the teacher:

1. Your story is strong in these ways: _____

_____

_____

_____

2. You could make your adventure story better by doing the following:_____

_____

_____

_____

Story Wheel

Cut out the story wheel. Use a paper clip as a spinner. Take a pencil and hold the paper clip at the center of the wheel. Give each student a chance to spin the pencil. When the pencil stops, that is the type of story that the student will write. Spend time in class sharing your stories.

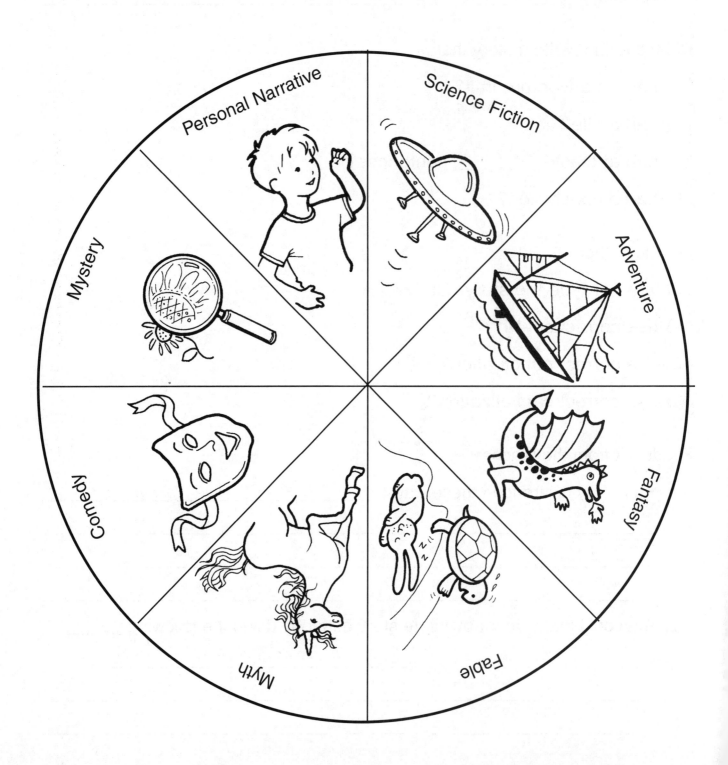

96

Story Writing
Assessment Rubric

Use the rubric below to assess student progress of the mechanics and grammar standards and benchmarks. The numbers and letters in parentheses correspond with the teacher checklist (pages 20 and 21) in the assessment section.

Competent

- ❏ The student can independently demonstrate competence in the writing process. (1)
- ❏ The student can independently use prewriting strategies to plan a story. (1A)
- ❏ The student can independently use strategies to draft a story. (1B)
- ❏ The student can independently use strategies to revise a story. (1B)
- ❏ The student can independently use strategies to edit a written story. (1C)
- ❏ The student can independently use strategies to publish a written story. (1C)
- ❏ The student can independently evaluate his/her own stories. (1D)
- ❏ The student can independently evaluate others' stories. (1D)
- ❏ The student can independently show competence in stylistic/rhetorical aspects of writing. (2)
- ❏ The student can independently use general, frequently used words to convey basic ideas. (2A)

Emergent

- ❏ The student can usually demonstrate competence in the writing process. (1)
- ❏ The student can usually use prewriting strategies to plan a story. (1A)
- ❏ The student can usually use strategies to draft a story. (1B)
- ❏ The student can usually use strategies to revise a story. (1B)
- ❏ The student can usually use strategies to edit a written story. (1C)
- ❏ The student can usually use strategies to publish a written story. (1C)
- ❏ The student can usually evaluate his/her own stories. (1D)
- ❏ The student can usually evaluate others' stories. (1D)
- ❏ The student can usually demonstrate competence in stylistic and rhetorical aspects of writing. (2)
- ❏ The student can usually use general, frequently used words to convey basic ideas. (2A)

Beginner

- ❏ The student requires assistance to demonstrate competence in the writing process. (1)
- ❏ The student requires assistance to use prewriting strategies to plan a story. (1A)
- ❏ The student requires assistance to use strategies to draft a story. (1B)
- ❏ The student requires assistance to use strategies to revise a story. (1B)
- ❏ The student requires assistance to use strategies to edit a written story. (1C)
- ❏ The student requires assistance to use strategies to publish a written story. (1C)
- ❏ The student requires assistance to evaluate his/her own stories. (1D)
- ❏ The student requires assistance to evaluate others' stories. (1D)
- ❏ The student requires assistance to show competence in stylistic/rhetorical aspects of writing. (2)
- ❏ The student requires assistance to use general, frequently used words to convey basic ideas. (2A)

Bring a Story to Life!

At this point in the unit, students have had the opportunity to write a large variety of stories. This section will give students a chance to bring those stories to life! Sharing the stories the students write is not only rewarding and fun; it can also teach the students about the audience to whom they are writing, as well as the quality of the stories they are writing.

This section of the unit has ten lessons to be used when bringing the stories to life! You may wish to add other lessons or activities that your class has grown to love. Be creative and solicit ideas from your students on how to share their written stories.

 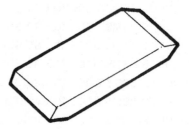

Standards and Benchmarks: 1C

Illustrate a Scene

Objective: The students will be able to incorporate illustrations or photos into a story.

Materials

- piece of white painting paper for each student
- watercolor paints for each student
- student portfolios
- smocks or aprons, if available, for students

Procedure

1. Part of writing a story is being able to visualize what one is writing about. This lesson will give each student an opportunity to bring to life the setting of a story he or she has written. Distribute the students' portfolios. Allow time for students to look through their portfolios. They should have a lot of stories to choose from. Have students each pick a story that they would like to illustrate using watercolor paints.

2. Have each student visualize a picture from the story. On a piece of scratch paper, students draw a plan of what they will paint. Distribute a piece of white painting paper to each student. Using the watercolor paints, students paint illustrations of scenes from their stories.

3. When students have finished, allow time for the paint to dry. When the paintings are dry, spend time sharing them as a class. As each student shares his or her painting, have him or her tell about the story that the painting is from. Encourage the rest of the class to be listening and to ask questions and provide positive feedback for the students.

4. Decide as a class how to display the artwork. You may choose to hang them from the ceiling or display them on the classroom walls, in the window, or in the hallway. On the back, have students write their names and the titles of their stories that the paintings are from.

Portfolio Piece

Have students write reflections about how they feel about their illustrations. Were they able to share the pictures they had in mind? Do their pictures help the readers understand their stories? What do they like about their paintings? What do they wish they could do differently? Place the reflections in the students' portfolios.

Assessment

- Check off publishing skill 1C on the teacher checklist (pages 20 and 21) and use "Bring a Story to Life! Assessment Rubric" (page 109) to assess student work.

Standards and Benchmarks: 1C

Real-Life Drama

Objective: The students will share finished products from their stories.

Materials

- stories written by children in your class
- white paper plates (one per student)
- cardboard tubes from paper towel rolls
- scissors
- glue
- contruction paper
- stapler
- markers

Procedure

1. Cut holes in the paper plates for eyes for each student. Ahead of time, select four or five stories that have been written by your students. Select stories that are interesting, have action, and can be adapted to a skit. Divide your class into small groups and assign a story to each group. (Groups will vary in number based on the number of characters in each story.)

2. Give students time to read and become familiar with the stories. Have the author read the story to the other group members and decide who will play which character. Students are now ready to make their paper-plate masks.

3. Distribute paper plates and paper towel tubes to the students. Press together one end of the paper towel tube and staple it to the paper plate. Then have students decorate their paper plates to look like a character in the story.

4. Let students cut out things such as hair, ears, noses, and mouths from construction paper and glue them to their masks. Use markers to add details such as eyebrows and freckles to the masks. Students are ready to put on the skit.

5. Set aside a time to present the story skits to the rest of the class. Have the author, you, or another student play the role of narrator. The narrator reads the story while the students (using their masks) play the roles and act out the actions of the characters in the story. You may even want to present these skits to another class in the school.

Assessment

- Check off publishing skill 1C on the teacher checklist (pages 20 and 21) and use "Bring a Story to Life! Assessment Rubric" (page 109) to assess student work.

Standards and Benchmarks: 1H

TV 'Toon Time

Objective: The students will present a story in a different format.

Materials

- small box (gelatin or pudding boxes work well) for each student
- adding machine tape
- two pencils per students
- crayons or colored pencils
- aluminum foil
- tape

Procedure

1. Ahead of time, cut a window in one side of a small, empty box for each child in your class. This hole needs to be the width of the adding machine tape.

2. Distribute the boxes to the students. Have students cover the box with aluminum foil and cut and fold the aluminum foil at the hole. Push the pencils through the sides of the box at the top and bottom. (You may wish to do this ahead of time for your students, as well.) See the illustration to the right.

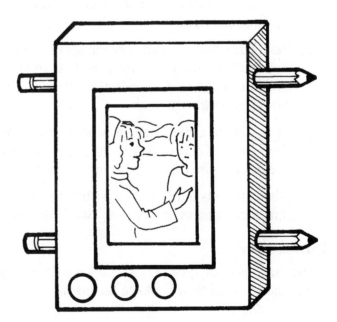

3. Distribute a section of the adding machine tape to each student. Students write and color the words and characters from a story of their choice. Tape the top of the adding machine tape to the top pencil. Tape the bottom of the strip to the bottom pencil. Then roll the pictures from top to bottom. Students read the story as they roll it and the illustrations through the box.

Assessment

- Check to see that students have put together their story televisions correctly.

- Check off publishing skill 1H on the teacher checklist (pages 20 and 21) and use "Bring a Story to Life! Assessment Rubric" (page 109) to assess student work.

Standards and Benchmarks: 4A, 4B

Become an Author

Objective: The students will be able to use books and information for research purposes to write a story about
an animal.

Materials

- multiple sheets of paper per student
- colored construction paper
- crayons or colored pencils
- long-arm stapler

Procedure

1. Schedule time in the library for students to have access to a variety of books about animals.
   Before going to the library, explain to students that they will be researching an animal to gather
   information for a nonfiction book. Have students select an animal they would like to write a story
   about. The books they read in the library will help them write an accurate story about the animal.

2. Allow plenty of time for the students to read books about their animals. Students may take down
   notes if they wish. Upon returning to the classroom, students can share with neighbors all the
   information they learned about their animals. Discussing the information will help students gather
   thoughts and key ideas for their stories.

3. Next, have students each write a draft for a story about their animal. Remind the students to write
   their stories about real animals and not imaginary animals. When they have finished the draft,
   have students reread and edit their stories. They may exchange their papers with a partner to get
   more feedback.

4. Next, distribute the sheets of paper to the students. Fold each paper in half. Students may need
   more paper. On each half of the paper, students will each write a sentence from their animal
   stories. Be sure they leave plenty of room for illustrations.

5. When students have finished writing the pages for their stories, have students select a piece of
   construction paper for a cover. Staple the cover to the storybook pages.

Portfolio Piece

Using crayons or colored pencils, students draw illustrations to go with the sentence(s) on the pages.
Have students read their books to the class.

Assessment

- Check off researching skills 4A and 4B on the teacher checklist (pages 20 and 21) and use
  "Bring a Story to Life! Assessment Rubric" (page 109) to assess student work.

Standards and Benchmarks: 1C

Puppet Stories

Objective: The students will share finished products from stories they have written.

Materials

- student portfolios
- construction paper
- scissors
- glue
- small brown paper bag
- yarn
- markers

Procedure

1. Divide students into groups of three to five. Distribute student portfolios and instruct students to look through their portfolios for a story that their group will use to put on a puppet show. Only one story can be picked. Once the story has been selected, have students decide which characters they would like to play. When the roles have been assigned, have students begin making their puppets.

2. Have students draw their puppet's nose, mouth, and eyes onto the bottom flap of the paper bag. Use the yarn to glue on as hair for the puppet.

3. Students put their hands inside the bags to move the puppets' mouths. Tongues can be added to the undersides of the flaps if desired.

4. Use scissors, construction paper, and markers to make things such as polka dots, bow ties, and buttons. Glue them onto the puppet.

5. When puppets are complete, each group can practice their puppet show story. They will need to rehearse this a few times. Talk with students about how to show feelings with a puppet. Let students practice showing happiness, sadness, excitement, anger, and so forth.

6. Turn a table over on its side, cut a puppet show stage from a large cardboard box, or make your own puppet show theater for the students to perform in. Invite another class to come and hear the puppet show stories.

Assessment

- Check off publishing skill 1C on the teacher checklist (pages 20 and 21) and use "Bring a Story to Life! Assessment Rubric" (page 109) to assess student work.

Standards and Benchmarks: 1H

Story Game

Objective: The students will be able to write a story in a variety of formats.

Materials

- copy of "Story Game Board" (page 105) for each student
- 10 index cards for each student
- small token for each student
- die for each group of three to four students

Procedure

1. Reproduce the game board shown on page 105 for every student. Students then select a story they have written and turn it into a game.

2. Students will be working in groups of three or four. Obtain small tokens and a die or a number cube for each group. When students receive their game boards, they are to color and decorate them with scenes and characters from their stories.

3. Distribute 10 index cards to each student. On index cards, students will write questions about their stories. These can be questions about the plots, the characters, the settings, the conflicts, or the resolution.

4. When students have their game boards and their questions ready, divide students into groups of three or four. They meet as a group with their stories, their game boards, and their questions. Students take turns playing each others' games. First, they read the story; then, they place their tokens on the game board. Students draw a card and answer the question about the story. If they answer it correctly, they roll the die and move forward that many spaces. The first player to the finish wins.

5. Students then switch game boards and play the next student's game. Students continue in this manner until all students have played each story game.

6. Have a discussion with your class after the game playing has been completed. What types of things made the games go well? Were the questions easy to read and understand? What improvements could be made in the games?

Assessment

- Circulate around the room to assist students as they play the game. Check to see that the questions students are asking are easy to understand and can be answered.

- Check off publishing skill 1H on the teacher checklist (pages 20 and 21) and use "Bring a Story to Life! Assessment Rubric" (page 109) to assess student work.

Story Game Board

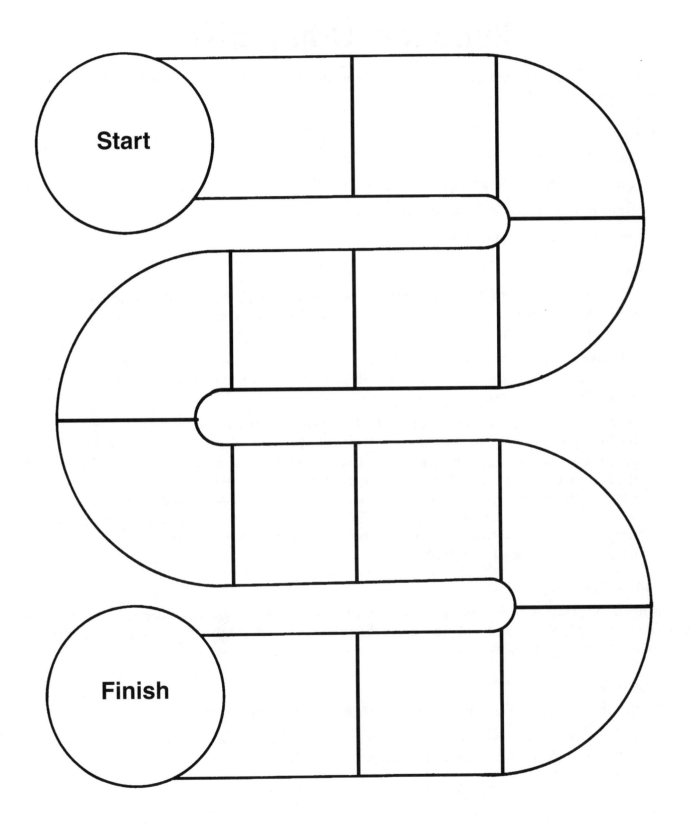

Standards and Benchmarks: 1F

Character Comparison

Objective: The students will write detailed descriptions of themselves and of characters from stories they have written.

Materials

- student portfolios
- copy of "Character Venn Diagram" (page 107) for each student
- white piece of paper for each student
- crayons, colored pencils, or markers

Procedure

1. Distribute student portfolios and allow time for students to look through their stories. Ask students, "Who is your favorite character?" Assist students in selecting a character that they can compare to themselves.

2. Distribute copies of "Character Venn Diagram" to the students. In one circle, students will write their names. In the other circle, students will each write the name of a character from one of the stories they have written.

3. In the circle with the student's name, students write down different characteristics about themselves. These may be descriptions, likes and dislikes, favorite activities, family members, etc. Then in the circle with the character's name, students fill in any information they know about the character. Encourage students to think back to their stories. What kinds of things did the character do? What type of person was he or she? Fill in those characteristics. Then turn students' attention to the middle section where the circles connect. Ask students to think about similarities between themselves and their characters. In what ways are they alike? Write these things in the section labeled "Both."

Portfolio Piece

Distribute the pieces of paper and have students write a letter to this character. What would they ask their characters? What would they want to tell their characters? When they have finished the letters, let students decorate the borders.

Assessment

- Check to see that students have completed their Venn diagrams correctly.
- Check off publishing skill 1F on the teacher checklist (pages 20 and 21) and use "Bring a Story to Life! Assessment Rubric" (page 109) to assess student work.

Character Venn Diagram

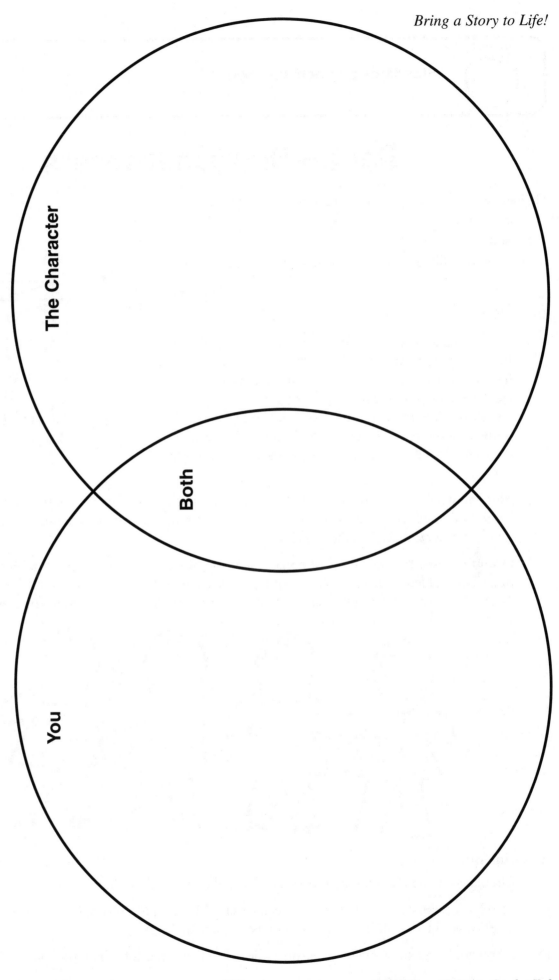

The Character

Both

You

Bring a Story to Life!

©*Teacher Created Materials, Inc.*

107

#2982 Story Writing—Grades K–2

Standards and Benchmarks: 1C

Paper-Doll Characters

Objective: The students will share a finished product.

Materials

- sheet of white paper for each student
- pencil
- scissors
- markers

Procedure

1. Have students select the stories that they would like to use for this project. They will be making the characters from the story. Distribute the sheet of paper to each student. Have students fold the paper lengthwise in fourths. (See the illustration on the right.) Use a pencil to draw the shape of a figure on the top fold of paper. (Make sure that the figure touches the folds on both sides in at least one place.)

2. You will need to demonstrate each step of how to make these paper dolls so that the dolls stay connected together. Students then use scissors to cut out the figure, keeping the folded edges intact in several places on the drawing.

3. Open the paper to show a row of dolls. Each one of these dolls will be a different character from one of the student's stories. They could even add themselves as the author of the story. Using the markers, students draw things such as clothing, hair, and faces on the paper figures.

Assessment

- Circulate around the room to assist students as they make their paper dolls.
- Check off publishing skill 1C on the teacher checklist (pages 20 and 21) and use "Bring a Story to Life! Assessment Rubric" (page 109) to assess student work.

(Note: You could use these character strips to decorate the border of a bulletin board.)

Bring a Story to Life!
Assessment Rubric

Use the rubric below to assess student progress of the drafting standards and benchmarks. The numbers and letters in parentheses correspond with the teacher checklist (pages 20 and 21) in the assessment section.

Competent

- ❏ The student can independently use strategies to edit and publish written work. (1C)
- ❏ The student can independently incorporate illustrations or photos into his or her work.
- ❏ The student can independently share a finished product.
- ❏ The student can independently write detailed descriptions of a familiar person and character. (1F)
- ❏ The student can independently write in a variety of formats. (1H)
- ❏ The student can independently gather and use information for research purposes. (4)
- ❏ The student can independently generate questions about topics of personal interest. (4A)
- ❏ The student can independently use books to gather information for research topics. (4B)

Emergent

- ❏ The student can usually use strategies to edit and publish written work. (1C)
- ❏ The student can usually incorporate illustrations or photos into his or her work.
- ❏ The student can usually share a finished product.
- ❏ The student can usually write detailed descriptions of a familiar person and character. (1F)
- ❏ The student can usually write in a variety of formats. (1H)
- ❏ The student can usually gather and use information for research purposes. (4)
- ❏ The student can usually generate questions about topics of personal interest. (4A)
- ❏ The student can usually use books to gather information for research topics. (4B)

Beginner

- ❏ The student requires assistance to use strategies to edit and publish written work. (1C)
- ❏ The student requires assistance to incorporate illustrations or photos into his or her work.
- ❏ The student requires assistance to share a finished product.
- ❏ The student requires assistance to write detailed descriptions of a familiar person and character. (1F)
- ❏ The student requires assistance to write in a variety of formats. (1H)
- ❏ The student requires assistance to gather and use information for research purposes. (4)
- ❏ The student requires assistance to generate questions about topics of personal interest. (4A)
- ❏ The student requires assistance to use books to gather information for research topics. (4B)

Story-Writing Learning Centers

Using learning centers in the classroom gives students opportunities to practice and reinforce writing skills.

This section has learning-center ideas and suggestions for teaching story writing. These learning centers can easily be altered to meet the needs of the students in your class.

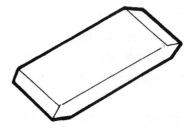

Story-Writing Learning Centers

Create a Setting

Materials—rectangular boxes, scissors, crayons or paints, glue, cardboard paper, construction paper, and any other materials

Procedure
1. Use the scissors to cut a peephole in the center of one side of the box.
2. Using the crayons, paint, glue, paper, and any other materials, each student decorates the inside of a box to look like the setting in his or her story.
3. Glue any characters and objects to the bottom and sides of the box. Have students look in the peephole to be sure everything is in place.

Story Time Line

Materials—paper, crayons or colored pencils, colored construction paper

Procedure
1. Instruct students to create time lines of the events in stories they have written. Using the crayons and/or colored pencils, students draw small illustrations to depict the events in their stories.
2. Students write brief descriptions about what happened in each event.
3. When finished, students glue their time lines to construction paper to frame them.

Life-Sized Characters

Materials—butcher paper, crayons or colored pencils, scissors, pencil

Procedure
1. Students think of a character from one of their stories they would like to bring to life. Pair students. One student lies on a large piece of butcher paper. As the student lies on the paper, the other student traces around his or her body. Then the students switch places.
2. With the scissors, students cut out the life-sized figures and color in the details of the character's face and clothes.

Dramatize a Part

Materials—dress-up clothes and/or props

Procedure
1. Students select characters from one of their stories. Students then select the clothes and/or items that would help portray their characters.
2. Students take turns listening to each other as they act out a part of the story that involves this character. Students listening may ask questions of the performing student.

Story-Writing Learning Centers *(cont.)*

Make a Book

Materials—white paper, construction paper, stapler, crayons or colored pencils, student portfolios (Ahead of time, make small books by stapling 4–5 pieces of white paper inside a piece of construction paper.)

Procedure

1. Have students select one of their stories to make into a children's book. Students write one sentence of their stories on each page of a book.

2. When students have finished the pages of the book, have students use crayons or colored pencils to illustrate each page.

3. Encourage students to decorate the cover, and they could add a dedication page as well, if space allows.

4. Schedule time for students to read their children's books to the class.

Bookmarks

Materials—copies of bookmarks on page 113, scissors, crayons or colored pencils

Procedure

1. Using crayons or colored pencils, students decorate bookmarks to go with the children's books they made in the previous learning center.

2. When students have finished their bookmarks, have them cut them out!

Travel Brochures

Materials—construction paper (one piece per student), crayons or colored pencils, magazines, sample travel brochures

Procedure

1. Fold the construction paper in thirds vertically. This will create a travel brochure shape.

2. Show students the sample travel brochures. Students will be making travel brochures to portray the settings and other scenes from one of their stories.

3. Students then decorate and color pictures of the settings from their stories inside the travel brochures.

Moving Mobiles

Materials—coat hanger for each student, construction paper, crayons or colored pencils, yarn, scissors

Procedure

1. Using the construction paper and crayons or colored pencils, students create the characters from one of their stories.

2. Students can also make items such as houses or cars that are also part of the stories.

3. Hang the characters and items from the coat hangers with the yarn.

Story-Writing Learning Centers *(cont.)*

Bookmarks

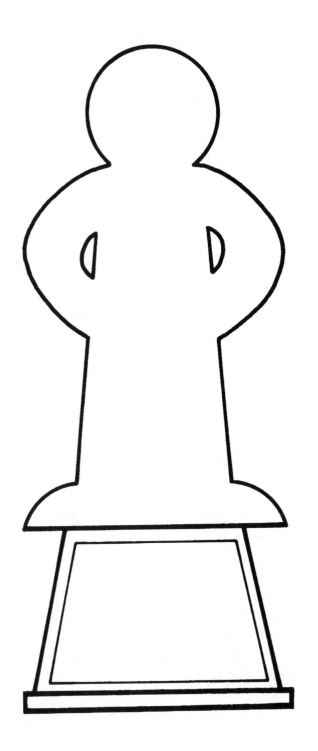

Story-Writing Learning Centers *(cont.)*

Newsworthy Stories

Materials—newspapers, copy of "In the News" (page 115) for each student, scissors, construction paper, and glue

Procedure

1. The students write stories using the newspaper format. To write these stories, the students have to answer the following questions in their stories: Who? What? When? Where? Why? How?

2. Have students use "Newspaper Stories" to write their stories. Then have students glue the papers to pieces of construction paper and decorate the borders with cut-up newspaper strips.

Most-Wanted Characters

Materials—copy of "Wanted" (page 116) for each student, crayons or markers, pencil

Procedure

1. Students select a character from one of their stories. Have students write down different details about their characters. They may read their stories again before doing the posters.

2. Students use markers or crayons to decorate and color their posters. Hang these posters around the classroom.

Letter from a Character

Materials—piece of paper for each student, crayons, markers, and/or colored pencils

Procedure

1. Students select a character from a story they have written. Students pretend they are that character and write a letter to somebody. They can write a letter to another character in the book, to the author, or to anyone else they wish.

2. After students have written their letters, they can decorate the borders with the crayons, colored pencils, and markers.

Rebus Stories

Materials—magazines, newspapers, scissors, piece of paper for each student, markers, and glue

Procedure

1. Using the magazines and newspapers, students cut out pictures that they will use in place of words. Students then arrange the pictures on the paper and write the words to their stories with the marker. The pictures are glued on in place of the words they represent.

2. Students continue until the stories are complete. Have students share their stories with other students and see whether the others can read and understand their stories.

Story-Writing Learning Centers *(cont.)*
Newspaper Stories

IN THE NEWS

Who?

What?

Where?

When?

Why?

How?

Story-Writing Learning Centers *(cont.)*

WANTED

Description of character:

Where the character was last seen:

Draw a picture of your character.

Story-Writing Learning Centers *(cont.)*

Postcards

Materials—large index cards, pencil, markers

Procedure

1. On one side of the postcard, students design and draw a picture of a setting from one of their stories. They can even write the name of the place across the top.
2. On the reverse side, students write a letter to a friend or family member, telling them all about the place or setting from their story.

Pentagon Stories

Materials—three copies of "Pentagon Stories" (page 118) for each student, crayons, pencil, scissors, and glue

Procedure

1. Distribute three copies of "Pentagon Stories" (page 118) to each student. In the center of each pentagon, students write a sentence from a story and illustrate a small scene to go with it. Do not draw or write outside of the pentagon. Each pentagon will have a different part of the story.
2. Students then cut out each pentagon and fold on the lines of the pentagon so that each fold faces up and the paper outside the fold points toward the blank side. Glue the pentagons together, matching the tabs to make a ball. The finished product should look like a ball with 12 sides.

Tape Your Story

Materials—cassette tapes for students (You will probably fit more than one author on one cassette.), tape player, stories written by students

Procedure

1. It's fun to hear a story read aloud by the author. Have students select one of their stories to read. Select a quiet spot for this activity. Students take turns taping themselves reading their own stories.
2. Each day, choose a different author to play his or her taped version of the story for the class.

Sequel!

Materials—stories written by the students, paper, pencil

Procedure

1. Working in small groups, students read a selected story to the group. Students listen to each story. They need to pick a story that they will write a sequel to. They can write a sequel to one of their own stories or a story written by another student in the group.
2. After students have finished drafting their sequels, they share them with the rest of the group.

Story-Writing Learning Centers *(cont.)*

Pentagon Stories

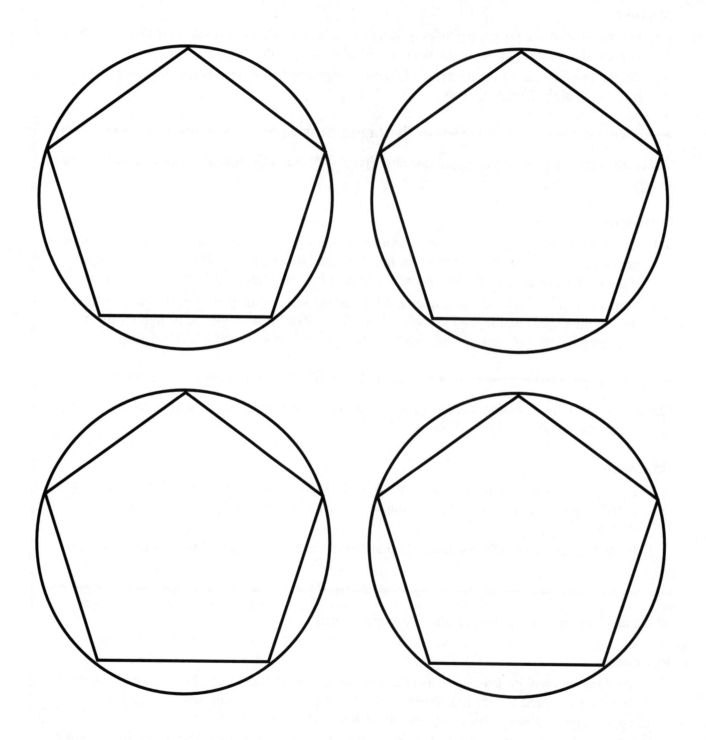

Mechanics
and
Grammar

This section of the unit is an optional section that you may pull from while teaching the writing process. You may find that your students need assistance in writing complete sentences or using nouns, verbs, adjectives, or adverbs in their writing. You may teach these lessons to the whole class, or you may teach small groups needing more individual instruction. Feel free to pick and choose from the lessons and activities in this section as needed.

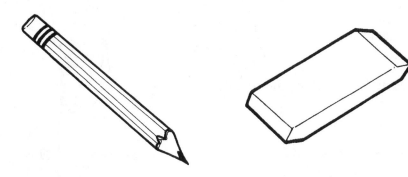

Punctuation and Parts of Speech

The following terms are used in this section of the story-writing unit. Use the guide below to assist students in learning and understanding the meanings of these words. These definitions fit the standards and objectives expected at the primary grade levels.

Declarative Sentences

These make a statement. They are also called "telling sentences."

Example: The boy is riding a bike.

Interrogative Sentences

These ask a question. They are also called "asking sentences" or questions.

Example: Are you going to the store?

Nouns

A noun is a person, place, or thing.

Examples: (person) *Sally* likes monkeys.

(place) *California* is where I live.

(thing) Where is my *umbrella*?

Verbs

A verb is the action part of the sentence.

Example: The dog *barked*.

Adjectives

An adjective describes a noun. An adjective is a describing word.

Example: The *green* truck came.

Adverbs

An adverb describes a verb.

Example: The girl ran *quickly*.

Period

A period is used at the end of a declarative or "telling" sentence.

Example: The elephant woke up.

Question Mark

A question mark is used at the end of an interrogative sentence or a question.

Example: Where are we going?

Comma

A comma is used in a series of words.

Example: I will bring the milk, cookies, and bread.

Standards and Benchmarks: 3A, 3B

Writing Complete Sentences

Objective: The students will be able to use complete sentences in written compositions.

Materials

- copy of "Complete Sentences" (page 122) for students
- class picture
- picture of a baby

Procedure

1. Hold up a picture of your class. Ask students to tell you what they know about this group of students. Have them share one sentence at a time. As they share a sentence, write it on the chalkboard. Do this until you have plenty of sentences to analyze. Next, using a different color of chalk, separate the noun or the naming word from the verb in each sentence with a line. Show students that complete sentences have two different parts. Explain how important both parts of the sentence are to understanding what we say to each other.

2. Using the sentences that students volunteered, erase the noun out of the sentence and read it. Ask students if the sentence makes sense. Next, erase the verb and read it. Once again, ask students if it is a clear thought. Are others who read the sentence going to know what it means?

3. Next, hold up a picture of a baby. Explain to them that as a baby, when they were first learning to speak, they used just one word at a time. But as they grew, they learned more and more words, and now they know how to speak in complete sentences. Have students turn to a buddy sitting next to them and say something that a baby might say and then say the same thing using a complete sentence. Explain to students that in our writing, we need to use complete sentences. If we don't use complete sentences, the person reading our writing is not going to know what we are trying to say.

4. Distribute the copies of "Complete Sentences." Have students complete the page. When they have finished, go over the answers together as a class. Circulate around the room to assist any children that may be having a difficult time with this concept.

Portfolio Piece

Hold up the picture of your class or another group of students and have students write three complete sentences about this picture. Have them share their sentences with a buddy. When they are finished, have students place their sentences in their portfolios.

Assessment

- Check to see that students have completed the page entitled "Complete Sentences" correctly.
- Check off the mechanics and grammar skills 3A and 3B on the teacher checklist (pages 20 and 21) and use "Mechanics and Grammar Assessment Rubric" (page 141) to assess student work.

Complete Sentences

What is a sentence? A sentence is a complete thought with a noun, a verb, and a punctuation mark at the end. Draw lines to match the groups of words to make sentences. Then write the sentences.

1. The children   plays the horn.
2. The man in the band   are having a parade.
3. I   begins at sunrise.
4. The new day   hope Grandma can see me.
5. Everyone   stalks the zebra.
6. The lion   smiles for the picture.

1. _____

_____

2. _____

_____

3. _____

_____

4. _____

_____

5. _____

_____

6. _____

_____

Write a sentence below about your favorite book.

_____

_____

_____

Standards and Benchmarks: 3A, 3C

Declarative Sentences

Objective: The students will be able to use declarative sentences in written compositions.

Materials

- jump rope
- copy of "Using Declarative Sentences" (page 124) for each student

Procedure

1. Hold up the jump rope and ask students to tell you what they know about this item. Write their sentences on the board. Be sure to place a period at the end of each sentence.

2. Now write the words *Declarative Sentence* on the chalkboard. Explain to students that they have just written a declarative sentence. Explain that *declarative* is a big word for a sentence that tells something about a person, place, or thing. The sentences they wrote were about a thing: the jump rope. This type of sentence always ends in a period (.).

3. Now do the same exercise with a student in your class. Invite students to write a declarative sentence about this person. Write their sentences on the chalkboard. Do the sentences end the same way as the sentences about the jump rope? (Yes, they all end in a period.)

4. Distribute copies of "Using Declarative Sentences" to the students. Have them write these declarative sentences.

Portfolio Piece

Have students select an object in the room about which they could write three declarative sentences. Have students write their sentences on a piece of paper. When students have finished, have each of them take a turn reading their declarative sentences and seeing if the other students can guess what the object is. Place these examples of declarative sentences in the student portfolios.

Assessment

- Check to see that students have completed the page entitled "Using Declarative Sentences" correctly.

- Read the three declarative sentences to see that students have written them correctly.

- Check off the mechanics and grammar skills 3A and 3C on the teacher checklist (pages 20 and 21) and use "Mechanics and Grammar Assessment Rubric" (page 141) to assess student work.

Using Declarative Sentences

A declarative sentence ends with a period. Draw a line under each declarative sentence. Then write the declarative sentences.

1. Jane and I sing songs.
   is the music

   _____

   _____

2. bees buzzing in my ear
   I hear the bees buzzing.

   _____

   _____

3. A monkey is in the parade.
   rings a bell

   _____

   _____

4. The animals live in the jungle.
   live all round here

   _____

   _____

5. and run in the grass
   Birds fly high in the sky.

   _____

   _____

6. I like the big book.
   So many books

   _____

   _____

Standards and Benchmarks: 3A, 3C

Interrogative Sentences

Objective: The students will be able to use interrogative sentences in written compositions.

Materials

- copy of "Using Interrogative Sentences" (page 126) for each student

Procedure

1. Tell students that you would like to play a game. Tell them you are thinking of something in the classroom, and they need to guess what it is by asking you questions. Select an object and have students begin asking questions. (Be sure to select an object that is not too easy to guess. You are trying to get as many questions as you can from your students.) As they ask you questions, write their questions on the chalkboard and answer them. Continue this way until a student guesses the correct answer.

2. Upon completion of the game, direct students to look at all the questions it took to guess this object. Ask students to look at each sentence. Ask them what they notice about the sentences. Some of the answers might include these: They are all questions; they all end in a question mark; and they all begin with words like *does*, *is*, *when*, *why*, *where*, *has*, *what*, *how*, *can*. Explain to students that all of the sentences on the board are questions and the fancy word for question sentences is interrogative sentences. An interrogative sentence asks a question, and it always ends in a question mark.

3. Distribute copies of the page "Using Interrogative Sentences" to the students. Circulate around the room to help students, as needed, complete the page. Go over the answers together as a class. Have students correct their own work by adding question marks and capital letters.

Portfolio Piece

Pick another object in the classroom. Tell students you would like them to guess it what it is. Have them write down at least five interrogative sentences to find out what it is. When students have completed their questions, read them aloud and answer them one at a time. Check to see that all sentences end in a question mark. See if students can guess the object. Have students place these samples of interrogative sentences in their portfolios.

Assessment

- Check to see that students have completed "Using Interrogative Sentences" correctly.

- Check off the mechanics and grammar skills 3A and 3C on the teacher checklist (pages 20 and 21) and use "Mechanics and Grammar Assessment Rubric" (page 141) to assess student work.

Using Interrogative Sentences

An interrogative sentence is a question or an asking sentence. A question ends with a question mark. Underline the questions. Write each question on the line.

1. Where the zoo is
   Where is the zoo?

   _____

   _____

2. Did you give Mom a kiss?
   box of games by the door

   _____

   _____

3. My friend is nice.
   Are you my friend?

   _____

   _____

4. Who is calling me?
   she is nice

   _____

   _____

5. The tree in our yard is tall.
   Are the flowers red?

   _____

   _____

6. Write a question about an animal on the line below.

   _____

   _____

Standards and Benchmarks: 3A, 3D

Nouns

Objective: The student will be able to use nouns in written compositions.

Materials

- index cards with "person," "place," or "thing" written on each
- copy of "Nouns" (page 128) for each student
- portfolios for students

Procedure

1. Tape the index cards across the top of the chalkboard in your classroom. Ask students to come up with words that fit into these categories. Write their responses under each category. Discuss with students what a *noun* is. Explain that a noun is a naming word in a sentence. A noun is a person, a place, or a thing. Using some of the nouns they listed on the chalkboard, make sentences to show students where the nouns are found in the sentences.

2. Divide your class into groups of two or three. Have them search the room for five examples of a person, five examples of a place, and five examples of a thing. Students may use objects in the room (books, maps, etc.) to find their nouns. Have students record their nouns on a piece of paper. Give students a specified amount of time. When the groups come back together, have them share the nouns that they came up with in their searches.

3. Next, have students each write a story independently that uses at least three of the nouns on their group list. Allow time for students to share their stories with their groups. Have the members of the group listen for three of the nouns on their lists.

4. Distribute the copies of "Nouns" and have students complete the page. Circulate around the room to see if students need assistance.

Portfolio Piece

Have students find pieces of writing in their portfolios and circle all of the nouns in them.

Assessment

- Check to see that students have completed the page entitled "Naming Words" correctly.
- Check off the mechanics and grammar skills 3A and 3D on the teacher checklist (pages 20 and 21) and use "Mechanics and Grammar Assessment Rubric" (page 141) to assess student work.

Naming Words

A noun is a person, place, or thing. Underline each noun in the sentences. Then write the nouns or the naming words on the lines.

1. Books are interesting.

   _____

2. Where is the store?

   _____

3. My kitten is small.

   _____

4. Is the class big?

   _____

5. Kim is six years old.

   _____

6. Is the park closed?

   _____

7. The teacher looks mad.

   _____

8. The story is long.

   _____

9. Write three sentences below and underline the naming words or nouns.

   _____

   _____

   _____

   _____

   _____

   _____

Standards and Benchmarks: 3A, 3E

Verbs

Objective: The students will be able to use verbs in written compositions.

Materials

- copy of "Verbs" (page 130) for each student
- portfolios for students

Procedure

1. Begin by asking all the things that students can do with their hands, feet, neck, legs, arms, etc. What are some of the actions that your body can do? (Some possible answers could include: jump, skip, swing, hop, walk, run, gallop, raise hand, etc.) List each of these words on the chalkboard. Explain to students that these are action words. Another name for these words is verbs. A verb is the action part of the sentence. The verb describes what the noun is doing.

2. Have students work with partners to brainstorm lists of verbs. Then have students select three of the verbs to use in a story. Students write the stories independently. When students have finished, let them read their stories aloud, with the rest of the class doing the action of the three verbs used in the story.

3. Distribute copies of "Vivid Verbs" and have students complete this page. Circulate around the room to help students, as needed.

Portfolio Piece

Have students pull out stories from their portfolios and underline all the verbs they can find in them.

Assessment

- Check to see that students have completed the page entitled "Vivid Verbs" correctly.
- Check off the mechanics and grammar skills 3A and 3E on the teacher checklist (pages 20 and 21) and use "Mechanics and Grammar Assessment Rubric" (page 141) to assess student work.

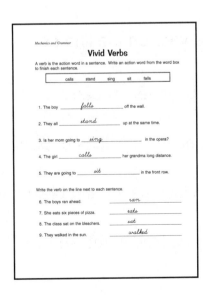

Vivid Verbs

A verb is the action word in a sentence. Write an action word from the word box to finish each sentence.

calls	stand	sing	sit	falls

1. The boy _____ off the wall.

2. They all _____ up at the same time.

3. Is her mom going to _____ in the opera?

4. The girl _____ her grandma long distance.

5. They are going to _____ in the front row.

Write the verb on the line next to each sentence.

6. The boys ran ahead. _____

7. She eats six pieces of pizza. _____

8. The class sat on the bleachers. _____

9. They walked in the sun. _____

Standards and Benchmarks: 3A, 3F

Adjectives

Objective: The students will be able to use adjectives in written compositions.

Materials

- copy of "What Are Adjectives?" (page 132) for each student
- copy of "Character Traits" (page 133) for each student
- catalogs or magazines
- glue
- scissors
- construction paper

Procedure

1. Divide your class into groups of three or four. Distribute a handful of magazines and catalogs to each group. Give each person in the group a piece of construction paper.

2. Have students select different people that they would like to describe from the magazines or catalogs. Students cut out pictures/characters and paste them to the center of the construction paper.

3. Then have students draw five lines extending from the person. Ask students to think of words they could use to describe this person. Explain to students that these describing words are called adjectives. Students then write five adjectives to describe the person. Post a copy of the page entitled "Character Traits" and discuss these with students to give them some ideas. Any time students can think of new adjectives to describe characters, have them add them to the list for future reference.

4. On the back, have the students write sentences using each of the adjectives. Provide time for students to share their work with the other students.

5. Distribute copies of "What Are Adjectives?" and have students complete them. Go over the answers together as a class. Provide assistance to those students who may need additional help.

Portfolio Piece

Using the person, the adjectives, and the sentences that the students completed, have each student write a story about this character. Allow time for students to share their stories with the class.

Assessment

- Check to see that students have completed "What Are Adjectives?" correctly.
- Check off the mechanics and grammar skills 3A and 3F on the teacher checklist (pages 20 and 21) and use "Mechanics and Grammar Assessment Rubric" (page 141) to assess student work.

What Are Adjectives?

An adjective is a describing word. An adjective is used to describe a person, a place, or a thing. Look at the italicized words in these sentences. They are adjectives.

The *tall* man walked across the street.

The *hungry* cat ate all the food.

The report was very *sloppy*.

The *cowardly* lion didn't have courage.

Adjectives give a clear picture of what you are telling about. Use the adjectives in the box to complete the sentences. Some sentences may have more than one adjective.

---

happy	tiny
wet	foolish

---

1. The boy is _____ they found his bike.

2. The _____ mouse poked his head out.

3. Three _____ children came in from the rain.

4. The man was _____ for giving the gold ring away.

5. Write an adjective in each blank to describe a character from a story.

_____ woman

_____ baby

_____ boy

Character Traits

The following words can be used to describe characters in a story.

Can you add to the list?

- lonely
- athletic
- selfish
- happy
- kind
- sweet
- gentle
- curious
- neat
- scared
- sad
- worried
- fearful
- cowardly
- thoughtful
- _____
- _____

- clever
- cautious
- wise
- enthusiastic
- apologetic
- sorry
- truthful
- friendly
- mean
- comfortable
- strong
- hardworking
- sensitive
- sloppy
- musical
- _____
- _____

Standards and Benchmarks: 3A, 3G

Adverbs

Objective: The students will be able to use adverbs in written compositions.

Materials

- copies of "Amazing Adverbs" and "Silly Stories" (pages 135 and 136) for each student
- index cards for each student
- paper and pencil for each team of students

Procedure

1. Hand out the page entitled "Amazing Adverbs." Go through examples of what an adverb is. Write some sentences on the board as examples and underline the adverbs. Have students volunteer other adverbs. Write their responses on the chalkboard. Work with students to complete the "Amazing Adverbs" worksheet. Check the answers together as a class.

2. Divide your classroom into teams of four or five. Distribute an index card to each student. Each student is to write an adverb on the index card. Place all of the index cards in a bowl and mix them together. Then pick a student from each team to draw exactly half of the index cards. Both teams have an equal number of cards as the members of the opposite team.

3. Set a time limit and have the teams each write a short story together, using the adverbs written on the index cards they have drawn. The first team to finish writing a story using each of the adverbs correctly is the winner. Read the story aloud to the class.

4. Continue playing this game to give practice using adverbs. You may use the same index cards or create new ones for each game.

5. Next, distribute a copy of "Silly Stories" (page 136) to students. Pair each student with a partner to complete this page together.

Portfolio Piece

Have students each write a letter to a friend who lives somewhere else, telling the friends about their school. Students are to use at least three adverbs (or more for some students) in their letters. Allow time for students to share their letters aloud with their partners. Store these letters in student portfolios.

Assessment

- Check to see that students have completed the pages entitled "Amazing Adverbs" and "Silly Stories" correctly.
- Read through the student letters and check for the three adverbs.
- Check off the mechanics and grammar skills 3A and 3G on the teacher checklist (pages 20 and 21) and use "Mechanics and Grammar Assessment Rubric" (page 141) to assess student work.

Amazing Adverbs

An adverb is a describing word. An adverb describes a verb.

Examples: The horse ran **quickly**.

Her stomach growled **loudly**.

I **quietly** walked.

The author wrote **quickly**.

Write the adverb that describes the underlined verb in each sentence.

1. Anne and Tom <u>worked</u> hard. _____

2. Elise and Erica <u>ate</u> quickly. _____

3. Ethan <u>listens</u> intently. _____

4. The horse <u>runs</u> fast. _____

5. Cows <u>eat</u> the grass slowly. _____

6. Mrs. Smith <u>yelled</u> loudly. _____

Write an adverb in each blank to describe the verb.

7. jumped _____

8. flew _____

9. skipped _____

10. slept _____

Silly Stories

Now that you have learned about sentences, nouns, verbs, adjectives, and adverbs, you are ready to use them in a story. Read the story below. Underline the nouns, verbs, adverbs, and adjectives.

Sailing Is Fun!

My dad asked me if I wanted to go sailing. I had never been before, and I was scared. But he said it was a perfect day. The wind was just right. I decided that I would like to go. We climbed into the boat and put on our life jackets. Dad pushed us away from the dock, and we were sailing! The boat went a lot faster than I thought it would. We almost tipped over, but we didn't. Dad told me to hang on tightly. We went all around the lake. I even saw some fish in the water. I wish I had brought my fishing pole. We spent most of the day in the boat. I decided that sailing wasn't that scary after all. It was a fun day!

Now work with a partner to fill in the blanks. Fill in the blanks with a noun, a verb, an adjective, or an adverb. Read your new silly story.

Sailing Is _____!

(adjective)

My dad asked me if I wanted to go _____. I had never been before,

(verb)

and I was _____. But, he said it was a _____ day. The wind

(adjective)   (adjective)

was just _____. I decided that I would like to _____.

(adjective)   (verb)

We climbed into the boat and put on our life jackets. Dad _____ us

(verb)

away from the dock, and we were sailing! The boat went a lot faster than I

thought it would. We almost _____ over, but we didn't. _____

(verb)   (noun person)

told me to hang on tightly. We went all around the lake. I even saw some

_____ in the water. I wish I had brought my _____.

(noun—thing)   (noun—thing)

We spent most of the day in the _____. I decided that sailing wasn't

(adverb)

that _____ after all. I was a _____ day!

(noun—thing)   (adjective)

Standards and Benchmarks: 3A, 3I

Capital Letters

Objective: The students will be able to use capital letters in first and last names and the first word in each sentence.

Materials

- copy of "Capitalization" (page 138) for students
- newspapers
- scissors, glue, highlighter markers, tape
- large piece of butcher paper with the words "First Name," "Last Name," "First Word in Sentence," and "Other" written on it

Procedure

1. Begin this lesson by putting your class into groups of three or four. Distribute newspapers, markers, and scissors to each group. Tell your students that you will be sending them on a scavenger hunt. Explain that they will be looking for capital letters. Ask your students if they know what a capital letter is. Ask for volunteers to share examples of when to use a capital letter. (The standard for this level is that students be able to use capital letters in first and last names and the first word of each sentence. However, some students may be aware of other times when capital letters are needed. Allow students to share these examples as well.)

2. Next, instruct the students to search throughout their newspapers for examples of capital letters. When they find a capital letter, have them highlight it. After they have highlighted a page, have them cut out the words and sentences with the capital letters. Students will then bring their words and sentences up to the butcher paper and tape them into the right category. After most students have had a chance to add words to your chart, have a discussion with the students on the importance of using capitalization in their writing. Look over the examples and have them make observations about the capital letters they found.

3. Distribute the copies of "Capitalization" to the students. This will give them more practice in using capital letters.

Portfolio Piece

Using the letters that students wrote to their friends (See the adverb lesson on page 134.), have the students circle all of the capital letters in it. If they see a letter that needs to be capitalized, have them correct it.

Assessment

- Check to see that students have completed the page entitled "Capitalization" correctly.
- Check off the mechanics and grammar skills 3A and 3I on the teacher checklist (pages 20 and 21) and use the "Mechanics and Grammar Assessment Rubric" (page 141) to assess student work.

Capitalization

Capital letters are used at the beginning of a sentence and at the beginning of the first and last names of people.

Examples:

> **I** hope you have read my story.
> **Is G**randma **J**ones in your car?
> **D**octor **K**enner is very nice.
> **W**e got a computer to use at home.

Write the sentences correctly. They are missing the capital letters.

1. where is the part about aliens?

   _____

2. saturday is my favorite day.

   _____

3. carol, are you coming to my house tonight?

   _____

4. i hope the dog doesn't bite.

   _____

5. uncle fred will be here tomorrow.

   _____

6. On the back of this paper, write a sentence that has two capital letters in it.

Standards and Benchmarks: 3A, 3J

Proper Punctuation

Objective: The students will be able to use periods, question marks, and commas in sentences.

Materials

- three 9" x 12" (23 cm x 30 cm) pieces of construction paper
- yarn
- copy of "Punctuation Mark____ ge 140) for students

Procedure

1. Begin the lesson by telling ____nts you will be discussing punctuation marks today. Review when to use the period, the ____ion mark, and commas in a series. Write examples of these being used in sentences on ____alkboard. Discuss with students how the voice changes when these punctuation marks ar____g used. Demonstrate a few examples of this, and then read some sentences together as a clas____nging the voice as needed. Distribute copies of "Punctuation Marks" for students to do. ____as needed. Check this page together as a class. Have students make corrections as needed.

2. Write a period, a question mark, and a comma each on a separate piece of construction paper. Tie yarn to them so they can be hung around a student's neck. Select three students to wear the punctuation signs. Now write on the chalkboard a sentence without any punctuation. Read the sentence aloud without any expression. Have the students who are wearing the signs come to the chalkboard and add their punctuation marks, if needed, to the sentence. Read another sentence. See if the students can add the punctuation marks correctly. (For students just beginning to understand punctuation—especially commas—you may want to tell them ahead of time which punctuation marks are used in each sentence.) Continue with this activity until all students have had a turn to wear a punctuation sign.

3. Ask for a volunteer to come up and write a sentence on the chalkboard. Have him or her leave off any punctuation marks needed in the sentence. Then have a student come and make needed corrections. Next, divide students into pairs. Assign one student to write a sentence needing punctuation, and then have the other student add punctuation marks. Then have partners switch roles. Circulate around the room during this time and work with students that may need further instruction, especially on when to use the comma.

Portfolio Piece

Using pieces of writing from their portfolios, students read aloud and use their voices and inflection to show the punctuation marks being used.

Assessment

- Check to see that students have completed "Punctuation Marks" correctly.
- Check off the mechanics and grammar skills 3A and 3J on the teacher checklist (pages 20 and 21) and use the "Mechanics and Grammar Assessment Rubric" (page 141) to assess student work.

Punctuation Marks

I want to go to the Desert Museum. Do you want to go too?

Periods and **question marks** are punctuation marks. They come at the ends of sentences. Write the sentences below correctly. Use the correct end mark for each sentence.

1. Is your book long

_____

2. I loved the book about dogs

_____

3. Can I write a story about you

_____

4. The plot is hard to understand

_____

I read a big book, a short book, and a mystery.

A **comma** is a punctuation mark used in a series of words in a sentence. Write the sentences correctly, putting commas where they should be.

5. I want to write a story about lions tigers and bears.

_____

6. Where are the library the office and the playground?

_____

7. Is the story a fable a comedy or a myth?

_____

Mechanics and Grammar
Assessment Rubric

Use the rubric below to assess student progress in using mechanics and grammar. The numbers and letters in parentheses correspond with the teacher checklist (pages 20 and 21) in the assessment section.

Competent

- ❏ The student can independently use grammatical and mechanical conventions in writing. (3)
- ❏ The student can independently form letters in print and space words and sentences. (3A)
- ❏ The student can independently use complete sentences in written compositions. (3B)
- ❏ The student can independently use declarative and interrogative sentences in writing. (3C)
- ❏ The student can independently use nouns in written compositions. (3D)
- ❏ The student can independently use verbs in written compositions. (3E)
- ❏ The student can independently use adjectives in written compositions. (3F)
- ❏ The student can independently use adverbs in written compositions. (3G)
- ❏ The student can independently use conventions of capitalization in written compositions. (3I)
- ❏ The student can independently use conventions of punctuation in written compositions. (3J)

Emergent

- ❏ The student can usually use grammatical and mechanical conventions in writing. (3)
- ❏ The student can usually form letters in print and space words and sentences. (3A)
- ❏ The student can usually use complete sentences in written compositions. (3B)
- ❏ The student can usually use declarative and interrogative sentences in writing. (3C)
- ❏ The student can usually use nouns in written compositions. (3D)
- ❏ The student can usually use verbs in written compositions. (3E)
- ❏ The student can usually use adjectives in written compositions. (3F)
- ❏ The student can usually use adverbs in written compositions. (3G)
- ❏ The student can usually use conventions of capitalization in written compositions. (3I)
- ❏ The student can usually use conventions of punctuation in written compositions. (3J)

Beginner

- ❏ The student requires assistance to use grammatical and mechanical conventions in writing. (3)
- ❏ The student requires assistance to form letters in print and space words and sentences. (3A)
- ❏ The student requires assistance to use complete sentences in written compositions. (3B)
- ❏ The student requires assistance to use declarative and interrogative sentences in writing. (3C)
- ❏ The student requires assistance to use nouns in written compositions. (3D)
- ❏ The student requires assistance to use verbs in written compositions. (3E)
- ❏ The student requires assistance to use adjectives in written compositions. (3F)
- ❏ The student requires assistance to use adverbs in written compositions. (3G)
- ❏ The student requires assistance to use conventions of capitalization in written compositions. (3I)
- ❏ The student requires assistance to use conventions of punctuation in written compositions. (3J)

Bibliography

Caulkins, Lucy. *The Art of Teaching Writing.* Heinemann, 1986.

Graves, Donald. *Children Want to Write.* Heinemann, 1982.

Graves, Donald and Virginia Stuart. *Write from the Start.* Dutton, 1985.

McClanahan, Elaine and Carolyn Wicks. *Future Force: Kids that Want to, Can and Do.* Griffin Publishing, 1994.

Sebranek, Patrick, Verne Meyer, and Dave Kemper. *Write Source 2000.* Write Source Educational Publishing House, 1992.

Silberman, Arlene. *Growing up Writing: Teaching Children to Write, Think, and Learn.* Time Books, 1989.

Adventure

Craig, Helen. *Angelina Ice Skates.* Trumpet Club, Inc., 1993.

Freeman, Don. *Dandelion.* Puffin Books, 1989.

McNaughton, Colin. *Suddenly!* Scholastic, Inc., 1994.

Scieszka, Jon and Lane Smith. *The True Story of the Three Little Pigs.* Penguin Books, 1991.

Steig, William. *Sylvester and the Magic Pebble.* Aladdin Paperbacks, 1987.

Viorst, Judith. *Alexander, Who's Not (Do you hear Me? I Mean It!) Going to Move.* Aladdin Paperbacks, 1988.

Comedic Stories

Graham, Alastair. *Down On the Funny Farm.* Random House, 1986.

Hargreaves, Roger. *Mr. Funny.* Price Stern Sloan Pub., 1997.

Hoberman, Mary Ann. *The Seven Silly Eaters.* Browndeer Press, 1997.

Stevenson, James. *Don't Make Me Laugh.* Farrar Straus & Giroux, 1999.

Fantasy

Joyce, William. *George Shrinks.* Harper Trophy, 1985.

Karlin, Nurit. *Abra Cadabra and the Tooth Witch.* Somerville House, 1999.

Munsch, Robert. *Paper Bag Princess.* Annick Press, 1980.

Mystery

Brown, Marc. *Arthur's Mystery Envelope.* Little Brown & Co., 1998.

Cushman, Doug. *Aunt Eater's Mystery Vacation.* HarperCollins, 1992.

Lewis, Beverly. *Backyard Bandit Mystery.* Bethany House, 1997.

Roy, Ron. *The Absent Author.* Random House Trade, 2000.

Tryon, Leslie. *Albert's Halloween: The Case of the Stolen Pumpkins.* Atheneum, 1998.

Bibliography *(cont.)*

Myths

Aardema, Verna. *Why Mosquitos Buzz in People's Ears.* Weston Woods, 1985.

Hobbs, Will. *Beardream.* Aladdin Paperbacks, 2000.

Kenneth, Steven. *The Bearer of Gifts.* Dial, 1998.

Steig, William. *Amos and Boris.* Farrar Straus & Giroux, 1971.

Science Fiction

Etra, Jonathan and Stephanie Spinner. *Aliens for Breakfast.* Library Binding, 1988.

Mayer, Mercer. *There's a Nightmare in my Closet.* Pied Piper Books, 1968.

McNaughton, Colin. *Here Come the Aliens!* Candlewick, 1997.

Stanley, George. *Who Invited the Aliens to My Slumber Party?* Aladdin Paperbacks, 1997.

Related Products from Teacher Created Materials

TCM #500—*Write All About It* (Grades 1, 2, 3)

TCM #2009—*Writing Workshop: Lessons and Activities for the Writing Process* (Grades K–3)

TCM #2494—*How to Write a Paragraph* (Grades 1–3)

TCM #2495—*How to Write a Story* (Grades 1–3)

TCM #2496—*How to Capitalize* (Grades 1–3)

TCM #2497—*How to Punctuate* (Grades 1–3)

TCM #2498—*How to Write a Sentence* (Grades 1–3)

Useful Web Sites

http://www.pacificnet.net/~johnr/aesop

—Many of Aesop's fables and their morals are available here; lesson plans are also included.

http://www.theteacherscorner.net/

—This page features a wide variety of lesson plans for teaching stories to younger children.

http://mgfx.com/kidlit/

—This Web page is designed for kids and includes student reviews of books and short stories written by kids.

http://www.track0.com/canteach/elementary/beginning.html

—This site has a story-writing game and other lesson plans that involve computer use.

http://www.educate.org.uk/teacher_zone/classroom/literacy/index.htm

—This site has sections geared to teach and reinforce sentence structure, grammar, and other writing skills. Included are lesson plans, worksheets, and interactive activities.

Answer Key

Get It Together (page 55)

The Lost Bone

There was a dog named Blue. He loved to chew on bones. One day he lost his bone. Blue looked and looked for his bone. He found the bone under the blanket!

Complete Sentences (page 122)

1. The children are having a parade.
2. The man in the band plays the horn.
3. I hope Grandma can see me.
4. The new day begins at sunrise.
5. Everyone smiles for the picture.
6. The lion stalks the zebra.

Using Declarative Sentences (page 124)

1. Jane and I sing songs.
2. I hear the bees buzzing.
3. A monkey is in the parade.
4. The animals live in the jungle.
5. Birds fly high in the sky.
6. I like the big book.

Using Interrogative Sentences (page 126)

1. Where is the zoo?
2. Did you give Mom a kiss?
3. Are you my friend?
4. Who is calling me?
5. Are the flowers red?
6. Answers will vary.

Nouns (page 128)

1. Books
2. store
3. kitten
4. class
5. Kim
6. park
7. teacher
8. story
9. Answers will vary.

Verbs (page 130)

1. fell
2. stand
3. sing
4. calls
5. sit
6. ran
7. eats
8. sat
9. walked

What Are Adjectives? (page 132)

1. happy
2. tiny
3. wet
4. foolish
5. Answers will vary.

Amazing Adverbs (page 135)

1. hard
2. quickly
3. intently
4. fast
5. slowly
6. loudly
7.–10. Answers will vary.

Silly Stories (page 136)

Answers will vary.

Capitalization (page 138)

1. Where is the part about aliens?
2. Saturday is my favorite day.
3. Carol, are you coming to my house tonight?
4. I hope the dog doesn't bite.
5. Uncle Fred will be here tomorrow.
6. Answers will vary.

Punctuation Marks (page 140)

1. Is your book long?
2. I loved the book about dogs.
3. Can I write a story about you?
4. The plot is hard to understand.
5. I want to write a story about lions, tigers, and bears.
6. Where are the library, the office, and the playground?
7. Is the story a fable, a comedy, or a myth?